PLACE 33
Part 1

In today's world, most people know about the existence of energy. Most people know that energy is a form of vibration. Most people have heard that, according to Albert Einstein's theory of relativity, everything in the entire universe is made from energy. Unfortunately, most people have not truly absorbed the most amazing implication of this discovery. Therefore, they have not made the effort to change their world view according to the fact that everything is energy

PLACE 33
SECRETS OF UNIVERSAL TRUTHS REVEALED
THROUGH HYPNOTIC CHANNELING (REVISED EDITION)

Copyright © 2013 Sherilyn Bridget Avalon.

All rights reserved. No part of this book may be used or reproduced by any means, graphic, electronic, or mechanical, including photocopying, recording, taping or by any information storage retrieval system without the written permission of the publisher, except in the case of brief quotations embodied in critical articles and reviews.

PLACE 33 PRESSES, LLC
Books may be ordered through booksellers or by contacting:

www.Place33.org
702.717.2137

Because of the dynamic nature of the Internet, any web addresses or links contained In this book may have changed since publication and may no longer be valid. The views Expressed in this work are solely those of the author and do not necessarily reflect the views of the publisher; and the publisher hereby disclaims any responsibility for them.
Any people depicted in stock imagery provided by Think stock are models, and such images are being used for illustrative purposes only.

Certain stock imagery © Think stock.

ISBN: 978-0-9915700-0-3 (sc)
ISBN: 978-0-9915700-2-7 (hc)
ISBN: 978-0-9915700-1-0 (ebk)

Library of Congress Control Number: 2013918806

Printed in the United States of America.

PLACE 33 PRESSES, LLC rev.
    Date 7/3/2019

Place 33

Secrets of Universal Truths Revealed
Through Hypnotic Channeling

Part 1

Sherilyn Bridget Avalon

Place 33 PRESSES, LLC
2019

Place 33, Secrets of Universal Truths Revealed

In loving memory of my grandfather

Gabriel Don Pingitore
March 15, 1910 - November 9, 1974

Sherilyn Bridget Avalon

Dedication

This book is dedicated to my wonderful husband, Keith, who is always there for me through thick and thin, through all the long hours of writing. I also want to acknowledge my four awesome children and seven terrific grandchildren: Trinity, Skyler, Navarra, Jienna, Zen, Lily, and Braden. You always inspire me to go beyond.

Place 33, Secrets of Universal Truths Revealed

Table of Contents

Acknowledgements 8

Foreword 9

Preface 11
    My Introduction to Hypnosis and Metaphysics 11

Introduction 12

Chapter 1 – The Beginning 16

Chapter 2 - The Elevator of Enlightenment 24

Chapter 3 - The Old Man 30

Chapter 4 – A Ghost In The Room 39

Chapter 5 - The Visitation 51

Chapter 6 - First Momentum 66

Chapter 7 - Look To The Left 78

Chapter 8 - Karmic Tar 84

Chapter 9 – Mysteries Revealed 105

Chapter 10 - Guardian of Egos 116

Chapter 11 – Mystery of Being 133

Chapter 12 – Ego Discord 145

Chapter 13 – They Hold The Cards 165

Chapter 14 – Margot Makes A Choice 172

Chapter 15 – Community of Neithertime 180

Chapter 16 – Magnetic Energy 197

Chapter 17 – Alpha Beta 203

Chapter 18 – Joseph and the Protoplasm 210

References 231

Acknowledgements

I am thankful for my beautiful Earth Mother and my Earth Father, and to my loving Step Father, my unending thanks to you.

To Joseph Campbell, an amazing, extremely emanating entity of personified knowledge that lived on earth and found a way to finish his transcendence creatively. All my Love to you.

To my exquisitely amazing Godmother Angie, and my Spiritual Godfather, St. Stephan, who changed my energy, which changed my life.

Most of all I would like to thank Frank, who taught me through pain, and in the end, switched to teaching through love.

Finally, my humblest thanks and gratitude to my spiritual guides and all the spiritual beings that helped and guided me on my journey.

Thanks to Denise Michaels, who helped me with my grammar and with putting my thoughts in order to make sense of it all. I am also thankful for her first editing service. I couldn't have done it without her. Thank you for your patience and guidance, your use of the editor's red pen.

I would like to give a special thanks to my amazing friends Heather Beiber for editing the final version of Place 33, Secrets of Universal Truths Revealed through Hypnotic Channeling.

Foreword

Here is the theme of greater spiritual knowledge from the higher dimensions. It lights up the reader with hope and gratitude. The action of the hypnosis moves one from despair to peace. It could be just a dream for the individual or it could be for us all.

Sherilyn Bridget Avalon

I ask that the highest powers be with us,
and the Truth be revealed

Preface

My Introduction to Hypnosis and Metaphysics

I consider myself fortunate to have studied with a great teacher who pioneered metaphysics and hypnotherapy in this century, the Reverend Donald E. Weldon. I began my early studies with the Reverend, founder of Creative Guidelines in the 1980s. I wanted to learn hypnosis or self-hypnosis to quit smoking at the time. The series of courses he offered were aimed at opening us up to a greater power, to our Higher Selves. The intention is for one to work with life instead of against it. Donald was the first to introduce me to what he called, "grow work." This is the method of studying order and discipline, which he embraced. He also taught me to send me Love to everyone, which helps people to embrace their highest good.

Through my own "grow work," he always said: "You must learn to crawl before you walk." I know I was always very impatient.

I have found the study of Quantum Physics explains it best. The biggest thing in our lives relates to the smallest thing in our lives. With the study of Quantum Entanglement, we can see how, and if, we are connecting with the other side.

Researchers have now isolated and studied "the God Particle." They have observed us doing what we do on the physical side simultaneously with the spiritual side, as they (we?) are observed through waves of electrons. Human observation decides what happens--or is it consciousness?

Introduction

A SPIRITUAL AWAKENING IN THE KINGDOM OF THE DIVINE MIND

Does the soul survive the death of the body? How do we know? What is a Soul? These are questions most of us ask throughout our lives.

People have been pronounced clinically dead, and after a few hours have come back to life. In recent years many of them have talked of "going to the light." During that experience they have seen and heard others familiar to them say, "It is not your time yet. There is something you have not yet completed back on Earth."

"Why? Is it just circumstance, or is there a reason? I have grappled with these questions ever since I was a young girl. How about you? Are you ready to expand your mind?"

This book is a story about my journey as a catalyst for Sterling.

It shares the story of an ultra expanded consciousness available to us all. Tapping into the super conscious mind of others now living on other dimensions and communicating directly to them through thought and the transmission of thought. It was amazing. I have experienced several past life regressions, but nothing like this.

No matter what your background or your beliefs regarding hypnosis, the narrative of the sessions is sure to expand your mind. They may even change the direction of your thoughts and your life. I cannot say exactly what led me to this amazing journey, but I know there was a reason I had to take the trip. I'm extremely grateful for the opportunity to learn the dynamics of the spiritual world. To give the story a little flair, I located the "Elevator of Enlightenment" at our wind tunnel, truly a manmade vortex of good intent.

Are you ready ? Enjoy the ride.

Place 33, Secrets of Universal Truths Revealed

*You don't have a soul. You are a soul.
You have a body. — C.S. Lewis*

Sherilyn Bridget Avalon

"Seek ye first the Kingdom of God and it's righteousness of thought and all else will be added unto you, and it was."
Sherilyn Bridget Avalon

The kingdom of God exists within you - Jesus
(Luke 17:21)

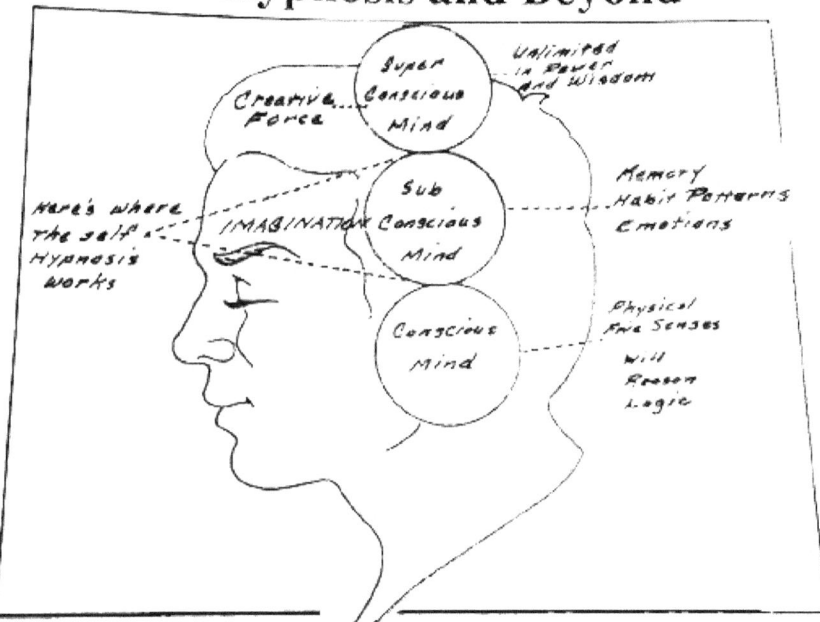

Chapter 1 – The Beginning

The morning light shone through a crack in the curtain. The fan was blowing the pages of a book on the hypnotherapist's desk. The room was bland. Lots of beige, no bright colors or accents. It felt like a doctors office.

Let's peer in on a session between Sherilyn and her hypnotherapist. She is distraught because her belief system has been compromised.

While under the influence of hypnosis, she tells the truth.

"Let's start from the beginning," her Therapist says. "How did it all start?"

"Okay," Sherilyn replies. "I always had an adventurous spirit. I read the book There is a River by Thomas Sugrue. The book was about Edgar Cayce who was an American psychic during the turn of the century. He possessed the ability to answer questions on subjects such as healing and wars. He also experienced visions of the world ending. He was a seer, and he would go into a hypnotic trance and heal others while seeing their spirit."

It was at that point in time I realized that's what I wanted to do. I had no idea what it meant. After being raised a devout Catholic/Christian, it opened my eyes to the possibilities of the other side of the veil."

Growing anxious about sharing her story Sherilyn says: "Okay, Okay look, when I first started coming here to these counseling sessions, it was just to humor my mother. Now I don't know if things are up or down, if this is real or not real.

It all started when my biological father entered a contest. An eccentric old man offered to give a prize of one million dollars to the person who could prove the existence of the soul. Dad got an honorable mention in that contest and was chosen as one of the people who had proof of a soul (in a way). His proof came from books. He said when an author writes something and you read it back, it brings forth the soul presence of the individual who wrote the book. That is, as long as the thought remains alive, then the Soul remains alive." The hypnotherapist found that a fascinating way to explain the existence of a Soul.

Place 33, Secrets of Universal Truths Revealed

"However, that's only one dimension of the riddle," Sherilyn concludes. "He also believed there was no such thing as an afterlife. Can you imagine? You're just dead and in darkness for eternity; that's it." Sherilyn wiggled in her seat while relaying this thought because it bothered her so much.

"My biological father left when I was very young, around two years old. I didn't have the opportunity to know him until later in life. Mother remarried and I then had a stepfather around the age of five. My Stepfather is a good man," Sherilyn says. "He just didn't know how to handle children. He did the best he could at the time I suppose. He did teach me to be entrepreneurial and always do my best."

"But, my Grandfather was always there for me as a child." She says enthusiastically.

She and her Grandpa were genuinely close. She loved him so much. Then she remembered, He always came to visit us on Wednesdays. He always brought pie and ice cream. Mom would cook a delicious homemade dinner, which he always enjoyed because he was divorced, and he didn't cook much. She also remembers running outdoors with her two brothers, knowing sunrise was about the time when he would show up. So they raced over to Grandpa's car to see who would get there fastest-- who would get the ice cream first?

When I was 15-years old, Grandpa took me on a trip to Lake Tahoe. He liked joking about how his brand-new sports car, a 1974 Chevrolet Camaro, was 'a chick magnet.' With a wink he would chuckle about how I would deter all the women who might be attracted to him and his sporty ride. We stayed with my cousins in their cabin at the lake. I was so excited and happy to see them because we had so much fun every time we got together.

This time was no exception. One night Grandpa and I visited the lounge at Harvey's. I should have been 21 to get into the lounge. Back then they were more lenient with the rules. She remembers feeling uncomfortable and nervous about sitting in a lounge, even with Grandpa. So, they sat way back in a corner booth. "Frankie Finale" was in his final act when the bartender handed Grandpa a note, which she still has.

It read, "Don't bite your fingernails, it's a dead giveaway." Being so embarrassed, I stopped biting my nails and quietly sipped on a soda. Nothing was said about it again. I just enjoyed hanging out with him no matter where we went.

Country legend Johnny Cash was playing in Lake Tahoe that weekend. I didn't get to see him, but saw Bob Hope and the comedian Lulu. Sean Connery was there, and Grandpa was so pleased to get his autograph. Her cousins saw Elvis and Liberace. It was the best trip ever, a once-in-a-lifetime vacation.

Then it was time to turn around and drive home. That's when I thought I might give Grandpa a heart attack on the way home from the trip, because he let me drive the first 100 miles on the highway. I was practicing to get a Learner's Permit soon.

On the first stretch of the trip the roads were curvy and winding. I received little instruction on what to do when a semi-truck heads straight for your car. So I swerved a little to the right almost to the edge of the cliff in the Nevada Mountains. My heart felt like it was pumping seventy beats per second. Grandpa's strong arms on the steering wheel helped pull me back into the lane. Then he asked me to pull over so he could pop one of his nitroglycerin pills. That was the first time I realized he took any kind of medication. He calmly said, "I will drive now." We finally made it home safely to Arizona in seven hours.

The Therapist was taking notes as fast as she can. Her glasses hanging low on her nose as she looks over them and says "Go on."

"Two years later...My Mom, who was pregnant (after ten years of trying to get pregnant), had a scare, before finally coming home from the hospital with her new baby boy. My little brother Mike, he was born face first. "It was early in the morning November 9, 1974, and I called Grandpa to invite him over for breakfast." Sherilyn stumbled over her words, "Grandpa you've got to come over and see Mom's new baby. He's adorable except for the bruises on his face. The bruises were from the forceps during the birth."

I adopted the statement, "Mike just wanted to see where he was going before he got here"--a little family humor.

Place 33, Secrets of Universal Truths Revealed

I was playing pool with my brother Walt. An hour passed by, then two hours, and finally three hours passed.

Grandpa never missed a chance to come over to our house, I thought. That was not like him at all. I was growing worried. Suddenly the phone rang. It was my uncle calling to tell us Grandpa was found dead, wrapped in a towel after getting out of the shower. He was lying halfway off his bed with his nitroglycerin pill bottle still in his hand. He could not get the childproof cap off to pop one of his pills.

Grandpa transcended that day. He had a weak heart, the doctor said. It may have been caused by rheumatic fever he had as a child.

I remembered crying and crying. That was my first experience with death. My wonderful Grandpa was gone. I knew I would never see him again. Grandpa would miss all the things they talked about, my first love, getting married, and having babies. I wanted him to be there for all of it. "He and I were tight," she exclaims, while crying hysterically. I was his only granddaughter and he always treated me like a princess.

My *hypnotherapists comes in reading over her notes,*

Obviously you felt certain you would never see or hear from him again--not so. It says here, years later you met a man in Sedona, Arizona whose name was Jananda. He told you that your Grandfather was with you all the time. After that encounter, you grew more fascinated with discovering more about the other side as many call it.

"Yes," Sherilyn replied. The Hypnotherapists told Sherilyn during her research She found an article in the National Enquirer, dated July 2, 1991 about a top surgeon, Dr. Sodaro, Chief Surgeon at Rome's main public hospital." The headline read, "I have no doubt our life does not end with death–I have scientific evidence to prove it!"

According to research by Dr. Antonio Aldo Sodaro, *40% of people who reach the threshold of death undergo a near death experience (NDE) in which they leave their bodies during a medical crisis.*

The article went on to say the surgeon/professor had

hypnotized 30 of his patients, and found unbelievable proof of life after death. "Hypnosis excludes the possibility that their recollections may be made up," he said. He also discovered people pass through four distinct phases during NDE's. First, a sense of calmness when they realize they are dead and they have left their body. While floating outside their bodies, they are drawn toward a heavenly light. Many resist the pull of the light and finally they return to stay on earth.

Sherilyn interjected, "I call it "**D**eparted **E**ntering **A**nother **D**imension" or what we commonly call, "dead."

"Another man, mentioned in the article," The therapist goes on to say. He talked about seeing his Grandpa Joe during his near death experience. Dr. Sodaro said, "A young man was killed in a car crash. He observed his lifeless body in the twisted wreck of the car. He did not understand the desperation of the people around. He felt totally calm and relaxed. Then he felt attracted to a warm, benevolent light and started going toward it. On his way to the light, he met his grandfather, who was with a woman he did not know. They told him, "It's not time for you to come here yet. Go back to your life. They are waiting for you."

The young man wanted to carry on to the light, but they persuaded him to abandon himself to the force pulling him back toward earth. When he was resuscitated, he described the encounter with his deceased Grandpa Joe and the woman. Residents from his neighborhood came out of their homes and gathered at the scene of the accident. One neighbor recognized his description of the woman as a neighbor who lived nearby. When they went to her house to tell her of the extraordinary encounter, they found the woman lying dead in her bed.

Sherilyn interjected, again "**D**eparted **E**ntering **A**nother **D**imension."

Another patient of Dr. Sodaro's went into cardiac arrest while having a pacemaker implanted. The Doctor later told the paramedics, "While he watched us desperately trying to resuscitate him on the operating table, he was frantically trying to tell us 'to leave him alone'." Dr. Sodaro recalled that when he finally succeeded in bringing him back to life, his first words were, "What the hell did you do that for? You snatched me away from paradise."

"Everyone is happy when they go through a near death experience and return, except those people who attempt to commit suicide," the Therapist says.

Dr. Sodaro said they have a strong anxiety and deep sadness... "But when they are brought back, they generally have a much more positive attitude about life and never try to commit suicide again."

Dr. Sodaro also wrote, "All NDE subjects improve their spiritual and social lives, become more generous, optimistic and more positive. They know this life is just a relatively brief experience that leads to a better existence."

Then Sherilyn talked about a book titled, The Quantum Mechanical Body, authored by Deepak Chopra who wrote, "The Universe is the physical body of Cosmic Consciousness and the laws of nature are its mind."

Some scientists compromise because their instincts or desires prompt them to hope that life goes on. They point to research being conducted with men and women who have survived near-death experiences. They also recount the testimonies of medical personnel who have observed individuals undergoing deathbed visions. Many scientists argue that while the statements from people who have experienced an NDE are subjective, other researchers insist such reports provide valuable clues to the dimensions of reality that lie beyond our physical death."

The Therapist states, "Many believe the 'level' you go to depends on what 'level' of Unity Consciousness one is resonating within." The levels move up and down simultaneously as we awaken more within Universal Consciousness.

"I believe there is a veil leading to the other side, which we can cross over through the aid of hypnosis," Sherilyn dictates. "I have arrived at the conclusion that right after you die, the real you is fully present. Where? Some call it Heaven, or Sheol, or maybe even Purgatory."

The Therapist then responds with, "There is no scientific evidence that we go to Heaven after we die. There is no evidence, except from those people who have had a near death experience or out of body experience.

The Bible, and other spiritual books written about crossing over 'beyond' the veil of the ego personality into higher dimensions, provides insight into this phenomenon. But that's it!"

"What about the teachings of Emanuel Swedenborg, an 18th century scientist, inventor and mystic. He traveled out-of-body, which allowed him to visit the afterlife realms," Sherilyn smiled. She believed this was possible.

The Therapist says, "Through hypnosis, I discovered there are 33 dimensions. I learned that I could actually guide a willing subject through dimensions, similar to the experience of author, Edgar Cayce."

So the Therapist hypnotized Sherilyn, and Sherilyn went on a journey into the unknown, where she finds there is a conscious afterlife. What seems to be the most important thing is seeking a higher level of connection with God/Source and its Oneness. It is like having a near-death experience through the use of hypnosis.

Sherilyn explains to the Therapist, "Here is the beginning of my story about the other side of the veil. With the help of Sterling, Angie, Frank, Joseph and Kenton, it will enlighten you to the existence of other dimensions in the universe,"

The Therapist states, "The Elevator of Enlightenment is a technique used in hypnosis; but it is also real, on the other side of the veil in the Divine Mind."

Sherilyn adds, *"Jesus said that the Kingdom of God is within."* The Therapist continues, saying, "Close your eyes and enjoy the ride."

Place 33, Secrets of Universal Truths Revealed

How does the Soul survive
the death of a brain and body?

Chapter 2 - The Elevator of Enlightenment

20 years in the future...sleeping soundly, I'm dreaming of an elevator lined with stainless steel walls. I look at the ivory buttons and get ready to press Level 33. Suddenly, I'm at Level 33 without even touching the buttons, as if my thoughts alone transported me the doors open and I see "The Place" in all its glory.

"It's beautiful," Sherilyn replied.

It's something I've never seen or experienced before. "The colors are so dazzling. Colors on Earth are dull compared to these brilliant hues." The flowers sway gently as I touch their velvety petals. The frequency is pure bliss. I'm thinking about the 33 Levels of Truth. I believe I've found the opening to the other side.

Abruptly, I'm jarred to consciousness, back to the real world rather than my lovely dream state. The phone is jangling, insisting I answer. my friend Rick is on the line. He is talking about a business that needs artwork done, an indoor skydiving place.

Rick McChesney says, "Go right over and ask for Kenton. He's the Manager. He's waiting for you to help him with this ad. He needs it done today!" he says emphatically.

As a diligent graphic artist who knows the importance of deadlines, and desperate to make a little more money, I jump out of bed, get ready, and drive there right away. My mom is visiting and I ask her to keep an eye on the kids for the morning.

It's a beautiful day. Before entering the building I see the indoor skydiving place. On the front a big banner reads, "Indoor Skydiving." *I think, I've driven by this place so many times wondering what it is,* I say to myself. *"Now I finally get to check it out. I'm excited!"*

I walk in, go to the front desk, and ask for Kenton. The receptionist looks at me and asks warmly, "What may I ask is your business?" She really seems nice and bubbly.

"Graphic design," I reply. "I was told Kenton needs an advertisement done."

Place 33, Secrets of Universal Truths Revealed

With a warm smile the cashier nods and goes down a hallway to get Kenton. I wait patiently, looking at a wall filled with pictures and awards.

Kenton comes out and greets me with a big, friendly smile. "Hi, I'm Kenton," he says. He's tall and handsome with beautiful blue-green eyes, a prominent nose, and positively luscious lips.

"Hi, I'm Sherilyn," I reply extending my hand. I notice the warmth of his handshake and his long, soft fingers. I think to myself... *He doesn't do much physical labor, kind of like a doctor's hands.*

I'm dressed in a red business suit. Kenton is sporting a white T-shirt with a big logo of "Vegas Indoor Skydiving" plastered on his chest and neat blue jeans. Vegas Indoor Skydiving is a casual, laid-back kind of place. Immediately I felt comfortable. I quietly reply, "Yes, I was referred by my friend Rick McChesney to do an ad for you."

For a moment Kenton looks at her inquisitively and then replies, "Oh yes, my good ol' buddy Rick. Excellent! Let's go into my office." He leads the way down a hall and turns into his office, a somewhat dark, private place back in a corner. It smells like potato chips and turkey sandwiches.

"Have a seat! You can sit right here," Kenton says with enthusiasm. He pulls a chair up for me and he sits in the other chair. Both chairs are on rollers. Slowly I roll over to his chair to show him my Graphic Artist portfolio. As I show him my work, he scoots his chair next to mine. Our knees touch and electricity bounces between them. Instantly I feel even more excited to show off my artwork. We seemed to share a vital connection, filling up with new energy. It was as if our past lives merged and we were meant to be together. I've never felt that connection before. "Let's keep going!" he says with another megawatt smile.

So they kept talking. Their knees kept touching. "I felt an instant tie to this man and I sensed that he felt it, too." Sherilyn says.

He stood up severing their knee-to-knee connection and says, "Y'know what? I really like you, um...your portfolio. I want you to do all our ads." He took a breath and continued, "I need to show you a special place in the tunnel first." (That's what he called it — the wind tunnel.) It seemed like he was in a rush to escort me around.

I followed him, and he led me down a set of stairs to a 'special room' in the basement.

"Wait a minute!" I exclaimed. "This is way too fast. I've been down this road before. My Momma told me to watch out for guys like you." Then I noticed an elevator. It looked like the one from my dream this morning. "Kenton must like me a lot to show me this, I mused silently."

He puts his hand out to lead me closer to the elevator. "Where would you like to go?" he asks.

"Go? Where does it go?" I inquires.

"This elevator goes to some incredible places," Kenton answered, keeping his eyes on Sherilyn.

I'm shocked and excited at the same time. As the elevator doors open, it becomes stunningly clear this is no ordinary elevator. "I'm surprised because the building only has two stories," I belt out, breaking our eye-to-eye connection. "Wait a minute. This is exactly like the elevator in the dream I had this morning."

Kenton nods his head and explains: "I dreamed a beautiful woman would enter my life, and I was supposed to show her the secret elevator, The Elevator of Enlightenment." He walks to the stainless steel doors of the elevator pointing and says, "This is The Elevator of Enlightenment. Enter the elevator and your eyes will be opened. It's like a mega-dimensional awareness chamber. Step inside and you'll step outside of time as we know it on Earth, and become aware of other dimensions. You'll never be the same. But be careful. There are rules. Only a privileged few get to see this elevator now until the change."

"It'll lead you to paranormal things, otherworldly things," he stated. "That's what I heard anyway," he chuckles, not really believing the stories he's heard. He watches Sherilyn intently, gauging her reaction.

I paused, "I can't believe my ears." As I absorb his words, I can sense the enormity of them reshaping every part of my being. "I'm slightly dazed." I quietly reply.

Place 33, Secrets of Universal Truths Revealed

Together we enter the elevator. The doors close. Kenton says, "Look around. It's like a vacuum — a capsule with an absence of air, although it's completely comfortable and secure. It's kind of like being in what I imagine a black hole might feel like."

Still stunned, the only word I can utter is, "Really?"

"It feels safe and impenetrable. The metallic walls have a golden hue. The buttons are cool to the touch like buttons on any elevator panel. However, these buttons are made of genuine ivory and gold. Black inlaid onyx numbers are nestled down into the ivory and emit a distinctive look of elegance." Kenton meticulously explains.

"Kind of like dominos," Sherilyn blurts out.

"The numbers march downward from one to 33 in five, vertical columns. Across the top row, from left to right, the numbers read one, nine, 17, 24 and 31. There are only three numbers in the fifth vertical column, 31, 32 and 33. There is a space for 34 but its left blank."

"Why are the numbers like that?" I ask Kenton.

"Because you can't go beyond Level 33 until the change occurs," he replied. "Level 34 is a safety zone right now, kind of like a safety net. That will change, though." Kenton said, holding up his hands using a soft cloth Kenton cleans up invisible dust on the golden elevator walls.

"What is the change? When will it occur?" I ask.

"We are on the precipice of an immense spiritual change. It's a cosmic thing I hear," Kenton explains. "First, there will be a cataclysmic event affecting the Earth, like a dot in a tidal wave. For beings on Earth, it will feel like it's exclusively happening only to them. That won't be the case, but it will feel that way. It will be a universal cosmic event experienced by all living things. It actually belongs to the infinite," he says. "You've heard of the December 2012 Harmonic Convergence?"

"Well, yes!" I reply. "That's come and gone already."

"No one knows exactly the time this colossal change will take place. It's a change that's more about thoughts, energy and souls rather than a physical thing happening to the Earth.

Don't personify it and you'll understand it better." He smiles again giving her a knowing wink.

I cleared my throat and continued. "Are extraterrestrials involved?"

"Mmm hmm, yes," he replies, "They are not what people think, though. We're right on the edge of this immense spiritual change. I say 'immense' for lack of a better word. It's a metaphysical change.... **more of a cosmic thing, because the change will be throughout the entire Universe.** It's not just on earth. It belongs to the infinite. On our Earthly plane, it will be just one small fragment of the entire shift." This will be a universal cosmic event interrelated among all things that exist.

"What will be affected by what happens?" I ask.

"Remember, we're talking about thoughts, energy and souls more than a physical change like an earthquake or a tsunami washing across the land," Kenton reiterates.

"I see. Are you talking about the second coming of Christ or maybe the Ascension?" I ask. "Are you saying people need to learn about it?" "Yes, yes. It's something we'll all participate in. Well; at least people who are more progressed. Actually, people who are more progressed already know, just as you do Sherilyn. You can feel it, can't you? I mean, you may not know exactly what it is, but you feel it, right? Our vibrational rate is accelerating."

"Yes, I definitely feel it. I constantly hear a ringing in my ears. How will it happen?" I ask.

Kenton replies, "You've heard how atoms and molecules explode when they're heated up, right? There is some activity, then more activity, then more, and more, and more activity until everything finally explodes!" He makes hand gestures of an explosion and scares me with a loud bang at the end.

"Sounds like what scientists call the Big Bang theory, how the Universe was created," I calmly state.

"Yeah, a constant expansion and contraction is happening. Everything is expanding and contracting from the vast Universe to the tiniest atom. Right down to the fundamental core. Everything's expanding and contracting, like breathing in and breathing out. Basically the expansion's no different from the

Place 33, Secrets of Universal Truths Revealed

contraction. Get far enough away from the process so you can visualize it and it's natural to ask questions like, what's actually upside down and what's truly right side up?" Kenton chuckles softly. "It just depends on how you look at it." He gazed at Sherilyn with those amazing blue-green eyes.

The moment is shattered as Kenton gets a text message on his cell phone. "I'm sorry, I have to take this, and we'll have to do this another time. They need me up front. Can you come back tomorrow?" he asks.

"Sure, I'll be finishing up your ad and give you a call tomorrow, when it's done." I smile as I reminisce about what I just learned.

"Great!" Kenton says, smiling back.
I walk out into the Las Vegas sunshine and to my car. I can't help but think of the spark between our knees and the world he's begun sharing with me. Driving home I reflect...*Wow! What a different kind of meeting that was, and what a fascinating man that Kenton is!*

Chapter 3 - The Old Man

2 Years earlier before moving to Las Vegas. We see Sherilyn talking with her hypnotherapist. Her therapist talked about her life, and how it had became a blur of the life she's now living, as if she was re-living every moment all over again.

"Ok," her therapist says, "let's start where we left off," Reading her notes…

We see a young, teen girl Sherilyn, at age 14. She ran away to Colorado with some bikers, because she thought her parents were too strict. Her stepfather was abusive. You wanted to be a free spirit. You had asthma as a child. It was winter, and the Colorado winter temperatures are sometimes below 30 degrees. You took ill with asthma, which forced you to come home after being away for a week.

"Your stepfather picked you up from the bus station, and then struck you for running away. This time he gave you a black eye and put you in a juvenile detention center for an extra week. It was two weeks until you saw your mother, a woman who came of age in the 1940's, that was in the era of spare the rod and spoil the child, a passive women who never stood up for herself. She lived in fear of her controlling husband you say."

"Yes," Sherilyn interjects, "Fear was always in her way."

"Do you feel your mother-daughter relationship would have been closer, if mom would have stood up for herself?" Her therapist asked.

"I was sorry for what I put my parents through after spending a week in Juvenile Detention." My mom said, "Run away again, and you're out of the house for good."

"Let me explain, Sherilyn goes on, It was a gorgeous summer morning the sky was like a turquoise blue and a pinkish peach behind the mountains, hinting that the sunrise was about ready to leave. On this day my friend Dana and I,
both age 16, missed the school bus we were going to summer school, so we started walking to school. A man pulled over

Place 33, Secrets of Universal Truths Revealed

with his girlfriend (or wife) in the car and said, "Do you want a ride? You girls look tired."

"Dana and I were tired and the hot Arizona sun was starting to come out." Sherilyn said with a sunny smile.

"They look safe. What do you think?" I asked Dana.

Dana said, "Sure, why not?"

"And so we got in the car. It didn't feel right," Sherilyn revealed. But, he did drop us off at school. The guy gave Dana his phone number and said he had a jet boat."

"Do you want to party this weekend at the lake?" He chuckled.

"We were excited. We had never been on a boat, let alone a jet-powered one. So after School we decided to call him.

We called him '*The Old Man*,' (an old biker term). He was older but we didn't know how much older. Actually we found out later he was almost 20 years older, as old as my stepfather. He lied and said he was ten years younger than his age. I was concerned about the age difference but Dana didn't seem to mind.

We were two teenage girls looking for adventure. That weekend Dana and I snuck down to the lake for the first time. We were both deprived of funds and this was the 1970's. After a long day of partying and skiing at the lake 'The Old Man' and his friends gave us some Quaaludes, two each to be exact! We had never taken prescription drugs before. So we didn't know what effect they would have on us. Yes, we had tried marijuana, but this was different. I was knocked out and couldn't move. Your body feels like rubber. Of course the deceptive, perverted 'Old Man' took advantage of both Dana and I," Sherilyn pauses.

"Upon awakening, I remembered what my parents said, "Run away again, and you're out of the house for good." So I called my mom the next morning and told her I fell asleep, which was why I didn't come home all night. Of course she didn't believe me. I was afraid to tell the truth for fear of being hit again."

"One more time and you're out!" bellowed in my head.

"You and your friend aren't allowed back here. Come get your clothes. They'll be on the front porch," she commanded. While practicing tough love.

"Alone at 16, I knew I could not stay at Dana's home. Much of the time Dana was already staying at my house because her parents couldn't handle her either. I heard about predators, but I didn't know much about them. I was about to find out. It was times like this I missed my grandfather.

So I asked 'The Old Man' if we could stay and clean his house for room and board. It was a new adventure right? Well, that is what I thought," Sherilyn exclaimed. "I kept going to school. I really wanted to get an education."

"I also started partying more and more. He and I 'The Old Man' became a couple, of sorts. We had an agreement you see, I cleaned the house, got more "'ludes" had sex and started smoking pot more often. If I stayed high, I figured it wouldn't matter that he was old enough to be my father.

"One day I came home from school and caught 'The Old Man' in the shower with another woman," Sherilyn hit her fist against the desk.

"What did you do?" Her therapists interjected.

"What could I do?" Sherilyn answered abruptly. "I thought I was trapped in this toxic relationship. *The Old Man* started bringing more young girls home with him to party. They were given Quaaludes, too. He was dealing drugs: cocaine, Quaaludes, and marijuana. Then we started having orgies. This was perfect for 'The Old Man' He had all these young girls and invited his friends to join in, too."

"While Dana and I were cleaning his house and felt like his slaves," Sherilyn starts crying. "What I thought was freedom from my strict parents," then she starts sobbing uncontrollably.

Her therapist finishes her sentence, "Turned into a Conquest from the Devil."

"Yes, some how I fell right into his lair," Sherilyn went on. "And then, one day I woke up vomiting. Oh my God, I couldn't keep any food down. My friends told me I might be pregnant. Then that's when I screamed. "Fxxk!" silently to myself. I cried myself to sleep that night."

Place 33, Secrets of Universal Truths Revealed

The Therapist says, "Go on"
Later that week I found *'The Old Man'* with my best friend Dana.

The Therapist commented, "I bet you had Feelings of betrayal."

Sherilyn looked at her and said, "ya think! I told that bitch to leave, and never come back. Then Dana returned to her parent's. I never saw her again after that. It really wasn't her fault. I realize now."

The Therapist interjected, "What about your mom? Have you talked to her in the meantime?"

"I had not talked with my Mom for months," Sherilyn cringed.

But, I had to call her; I had to tell her I wanted to marry this guy. I was pregnant. Because I was under age 18, my parents needed to sign documents to give me the rights to become an underage bride. I was rebellious, and hardheaded and still angry with my mother for kicking me out of the house. My mother signed the papers. I married 'The Old Man.'

Her Therapist says, "You must have felt a little more secure."

"Ha," Sherilyn laughs. "On our honeymoon we went to Vail, Colorado and rented a couple cabins with the maid of honor and her friend, Danny. I was about 3 months pregnant. After the long trip I decide to take a shower. I took a shower, left the water running, and walked out to find my new husband making out with the maid of honor. He gave her Quaaludes; of course I quit taking the drugs when I discovered I was pregnant. *'The Old Man'* and the maid of honor were mad as hell that they were caught."

Her Therapist interjects, "The honeymoon was over?"

"Yes, but I knew what he was when I married him."
Sherilyn says in a somber voice, "I felt trapped! I started growing more cynical and decided to go out with his younger friends. He didn't know. *'The Old Man'* slept with different women all the time. I accepted it because I had a roof over my head. I had too.

Then I gave birth to a beautiful baby boy, Dallas. Now I had an infant son to care for along with cleaning the house. I grew used to the sex and started feeling closer to *The Old Man*. He was a construction worker and a drug dealer. I made him lunch at four o'clock in the morning and drove him to and from work. We only had one car.

Then he bought me a car, an old 1959 Cadillac. I was 17, it was the late 70's, and I quit school and got a job at the "Hansel and Gretel" daycare down the street. One day, at 4 o'clock in the afternoon, a car rear-ended me going 65 miles an hour. The 1959 Cadillac was a heavy car. I was at a dead stop and the wheel was turned to make a left turn into the parking lot. The drunk driver hit the Cadillac from behind, then the car shot forward. There was a bar under the seat that moved the seat backward and then forward. Upon impact, the seat slid all the way back about 2 feet, I'm Petite, and I couldn't reach the brakes. So the car sailed right through the daycare building. Bricks came through the front windshield hit me in the head.

Most of the time the children stood in front of the front door waiting for their parents to pick them up. Five minutes before my car hit the door, the children were moved to the backyard to play. 'Thank God! I could not have lived with myself, if I had hurt or killed any of those kids. (I believe it was Divine Intervention)

My son, then nine-months-old, Dallas was strapped in the car seat, but the seat belt came undone. Still strapped into the infant car seat, he flew up in the air, over the seat, and landed upside-down on the back seat floorboards. Everything happened as if in slow motion. The car entered the building. Glass shattered. Bricks flew through the windshield. My arm and collarbone were broken. I was also left with intense whiplash, but all I could think about was my baby.

As soon as the crash stopped, I jumped over the car seat picking up the infant seat with pure adrenaline force, not knowing my wrist was broken. Blood was coming from Dallas's nose. "God, please let him be okay," I cried.

"Then, 'The Old Man' was driving home from work. He saw my car lodged in the wall of the nursery school. Paramedics arrived on the scene. Despite all the commotion, I felt afraid of

Place 33, Secrets of Universal Truths Revealed

'The Old Man' I thought he would be angry with me because I wrecked his car.

Luckily I escaped with few injuries. Dallas checked out fine with only a little bloody nose. It was as if the angels held him in place when he flipped over the car seat as the seat went backwards.

A personal injury lawsuit was filed. I received a check for $75,000. *'The Old Man'* bought property with it. I put a little money away every day. I knew the marriage would not last much longer. I was growing stronger as a young, woman. I was maturing I guess.

'The Old Man' and I had another beautiful boy named, Dillon. I could feel I was changing. The cruel words he said daily like "you're not good enough, you're not good-looking, you'll never do anything in your life" started to dissipate. *'The Old Man'* got into real estate and started buying properties. I was taking care of my sons. Life was almost good." Sherilyn says with a sigh.

Her Therapist interjects, "it seems like your growing to love The Old Man"

"It was an illusion!" Sherilyn sarcastically says, "the illusion of the good life was destroyed one night when I went out with my friends from high school, I came home late. I'll admit I drank a little too much. I walked in the house. The lights were out and *'The Old Man'* was sitting in his Lazy Boy chair in the dark. He scared the shit out of me when he yelled, "Where the hell have you been?" I felt washed over with the same fear I felt when my stepdad yelled before hitting me." Sherilyn went on.

"That evening *'The Old Man'* watched the children for the first time ever. Three-month-old Dillon cried for three hours straight, he informed me. (*No cell phones back then*) Suddenly he got up from the Lazy Boy and slapped me across the face. I ran into the kids' bedroom, crying."

He ran in after me shouting, "You bitch! I'm not paying for everything so you can go slutting around with your friends." He slapped me over, and over. Finally, I grabbed the baby and ran Into the bathroom, locking the door. "You're an asshole!" I screamed through the door. "I have no idea what you're talking about. We just drank a few beers!"

"I think it's time to leave," I told him "I really needed a break." He hit me before but it was back when I was on Quaaludes and did not feel much.

I quit taking drugs a while ago. Over time my head was becoming clearer and I had a secret bank account. The statements were mailed to my mom's house. My mom and I had a better relationship now. I missed her, especially at times like this.

I was almost 20 years old now I figured it was time to do what I wanted to do finally. I don't have to stay tied to *'This Old Man'* the rest of my life and be controlled by him. Why was I so stupid?

I need to take control. Dallas was sleeping. So I thought I could climb through the bathroom window. I am only five feet, tall and weighed a mere 85 pounds. I maneuvered myself through the window with my 3-month-old baby Dillon, running, walking, and hiding all the way to my Mom's house. My Mom lived a couple miles away. This time she helped me get away, and was somewhat sympathetic to my situation."

Her Therapist interjects, "You must have been terrified."

"Mm hmm, I divorced him that summer and got half of everything, which really made him mad. He was determined to ruin my life. I told him I didn't want anything. But the attorneys said you deserve ½ of everything. So I took it.

I realized I have made a big mistake, but I love my sons. They were the best things that ever happened to me."

Wide-eyed, the Therapist replied, "Wow!"

"I don't hate *The Old Man*, or My Step Father, or Mother" Sherilyn says. "I thank them for the life lessons. That's what I needed to learn at the time, and grow up to become the person I am today."

Her Therapist looked at her watch, "well times up for today." I leave and thank the Therapist.

The Therapist is sitting at her desk speaking into a microphone. She's dictating Sherilyn's session results.

"The Old Man wanted her to pay for her mistakes." Her Therapists rambles on, "When the boys were about six, and eight years old, he refused to pay child support when he quit working.

Place 33, Secrets of Universal Truths Revealed

He sued her for custody of Dallas and Dillon and won. He had more money to fight her and an attorney. While working at a real estate office as a receptionist, she could not afford an attorney. The job did not pay much. She got visitation on the weekends and holidays. She missed her children and cried herself to sleep every night.

Sherilyn is a 38-year-old who enjoys painting, watching television, and meditation. She is considerate and kind, but can also be very wild and a bit fun.

She is addicted to knowledge, something that her friend Dana Reynolds pointed out when she was 15. The problem intensified in 1998. When she met Kenton and Sterling.

She is 53 % Italian, 11 % Irish and a mish mosh of other various nationalities. She started Art College but never finished the course. She is allergic to Love.

Physically, Sherilyn is in pretty good shape. She is short about 5 ft. tall, but tells everyone she's taller. With olive skin, Auburn red hair and green eyes. Her eyes are slightly far apart but sparkle when she smiles. She is beautiful and witty but she has sadness about her. She has a heart shaped face, a slight cleft in her chin, full lips, a pug nose.

Due to the crystals she carries, Sherilyn looks younger than her actual age. She grew up in a working class neighborhood. Her mother kicked her out of the house when she was 16, leaving her with her own ideas to figure out life.

Sherilyn's best friend is a benevolent soul called Sterling Reynolds. They have a very fiery friendship. She also hangs around with Kenton Smith and Joseph Campbell. They enjoy a lot of conversations together. But, the weird thing is, Joseph Campbell is dead.

Sherilyn saved enough of her money to buy a Macintosh computer. She went to graphic design school and started working from home. She did typesetting for different print shops. She also learned a program called Photoshop, and started teaching others how to design brochures at AlphaGraphics. Sherilyn's future is starting to look brighter and I'm hoping she will find happiness one day.

Sherilyn Bridget Avalon

Sherilyn says, "She has learned to face her demons. Through all of her life lessons first and foremost, she must learn to always trust her feelings and there are no coincidences. If you watch you can see the synchronicity all around you."

Place 33, Secrets of Universal Truths Revealed

Chapter 4 – A Ghost In The Room

Sherilyn had two daughters by a new boyfriend she met a few years prior. She brought her daughters with her to Vegas.

"Go take your bath; then I'll read you a story." She tells her daughters. Exhausted from a long day of looking for a job, She lays on the couch for a minute. A country music tune is playing on the radio; about a woman and her children getting kicked out of their house.

She is falling asleep...She's dreaming about her guardian angel. She's under this beautiful tree. "I think it's the Tree of Life. She is writing in this book, I'm listening to her words" Sherilyn states.

Her guardian angel is reading, "Sherilyn tucks the children into bed, she feels sad about leaving her boys behind with their father. She misses them so much. But she has to be strong for her daughters now. Holding back her tears, she knows she will be with her boys again one day. She's pondering on how she attracted the same type of man again." Sherilyn fades off to sleep.

Her daughter Margot is eight years old. She has long-brown hair, beautiful and enormous hazel eyes, an adorable little pug nose, and a gorgeous smile. She loves being in nature. She has suffered with asthma since she was two, so she is a little small for her age, very petite like Sherilyn. Margot is a clever, lovely, little girl.

Her younger daughter Sally is five years old. She has long blonde hair and big bluish-hazel eyes. She adores her hamsters and bunnies. She looks like a little angel, and she has the disposition of one too.

Sherilyn recently left her hometown in Arizona, and her ex-boyfriend is stalking her. She felt she had no choice but to run away with the two girls. The night before, she had a horrible argument. He actually threatened to kill her. He said, "I'll cut your body into little pieces, boil the meat, and then feed it to the dogs. Then there would be no evidence."

That was the last straw. She had to leave. She couldn't take it anymore. Right now they are in a hotel room in Vegas, room number 333. It's the best she could do right now for her daughters. She figures she will go back to get her boys once she gets settled. At least they were safe for now. She's trying to build a new life for herself after years of abuse. Honestly, the relationship with her ex soured her on the possibility of a real, lifelong love."

Sherilyn awoke, startled, very early in the middle of the night. She saw a shadowy presence looking over her from the foot of her bed.

The alarm clock reads 2:00 am. "Maybe I was just dreaming," she pinched herself. "No, it is real!" She closed her eyes then the presence was gone. It appeared somewhere between her dreaming and awakened state, she concluded to herself.

Later, as she's sipping her morning coffee, she remembers dreaming of her Guardian Angel and cries out, "Oh shoot! Then there was a ghost in the room last night."

She kept hearing odd noises in the bathroom the day before too, but nothing was there. She decided she must go to the wind tunnel and the Elevator of Enlightenment today.

She thought…*maybe the Elevator of Enlightenment has the answer she is looking for? Maybe it will know what was tapping on the bathroom pipes. What could the presence and the noises possibly be?* She was afraid for her daughters. She remembers Kenton saying the Elevator knows paranormal things.

"Okay baby dolls, I'm dropping you off at school now! Mommy's got to work today." She gives each of her darling daughters a kiss goodbye. She makes a point to always tell them she loves them every morning and night.

After Sherilyn drops the kids off at school, she decides to drive over to the Elevator of Enlightenment in the basement of "Vegas Indoor Skydiving" to ask about the presence in her room — #333 in the Hampton Inn Suites Hotel.

First she must return to the hotel room to finish the advertisement as promised for Mr. Indoor Skydiving. "I can't wait to see him again," she says. "It's finished! Voila!" she

Place 33, Secrets of Universal Truths Revealed

exclaims with pride to herself. She jumps up and back in the truck and drives to the wind tunnel.

As she walks in, the customers who will soon be skydiving indoors gather, watching other people fly on the TV monitor affixed to the wall. Scooting past them, she sneaks down the back hallway then down to the basement. She runs into a guy with a name-tag sewn into his shirt that says 'TONY.' They smile and exchange greetings.

"I'm looking for Kenton," she says.

"Uh, oh. Okay, yeah, he's with a client showing them the wind tunnel," he stated.

"He asked me to wait for him by the elevator," Sherilyn says sheepishly.

"Oh, okay, cool!" replies Tony with a smile.

He seems a little bewildered, so probably doesn't notice her as she slips past him. She walked downstairs to the secret Elevator of Enlightenment. She needs to know what happened. What was the tapping on the pipes? "I probably should change rooms. I will change rooms," she decides as she mumbles to herself; flip flopping back and forth in her mind.

Glancing around, she pushed the classified button with the secret symbol just as Kenton did yesterday. He did not know she was watching when he entered the code. With a quiet *whoosh* the elevator doors open. She scurries inside, hoping no one is watching. There's a loud boom and suddenly someone appears in the elevator. It scares her half to death! She steps back out of the elevator.

"Who are you?" she demands.

"I'm Sterling, 'Guardian of the Elevator of Enlightenment.' I reflect the pool of knowledge," he says.

"Um, I didn't know there was a guardian of the Elevator of Enlightenment." Sherilyn says with confusion.

"Nah, I'm just the janitor around here!" he says, smiling. "What can I help you with?"

The elevator smells of lilacs and cotton candy. A silvery white light trickled through the elevator shaft from above shining on Sterling's hair. Sterling is very handsome with steel blue eyes and some would say premature greying. But, his hair looked silver to me. It is shoulder length and he looks like sterling silver. "That's probably how he got his name," Sherilyn was thinking.

"I'm Sherilyn. I'm here because Kenton told me the elevator would show paranormal things. There was a ghost in my room last night and I want to know why? Or, I'd like to know who she is paranormally?"

"Can't you just see a psychic for that Sherilyn?" Sterling replies, smirking.

"Well, I suppose," she says, still wanting to find the answer through the elevator.

He ponders awhile, almost as if he knows her and they are old friends. He focuses on her face when he blurts out, "Are you ready for an adventure?"

She nods eagerly and steps back into the elevator. Then he instructs her to push the button to go to Level 14.

"Wait! I haven't been anywhere in the elevator before!" she says.

Concern must have registered on her face as Sterling says: "Let's fill ourselves with white light. Relax your inner mind and let's see where it takes us."

The elevator doors close tight. Sherilyn pushes the button and off they go, swiftly to Level 14 with a *whoosh*.

"Here we are, Level 14," Sterling announces. "It's called 'The City of Movement.' It's a place of wishes."

"I guess that's what I need," Sherilyn says "a wish! I wish there wasn't a ghost in my hotel room," she answers.

"First, let's go to the place you're from, Place 33," Sterling says.

Sherilyn presses the button for Level 33. Instantaneously the elevator goes down and the doors open.

Sterling looks up and says, "As you look out you'll see that your whole world has changed. We've actually traveled to another dimension."

"Oh my!" Sherilyn shouted, "This is amazing!"

"We're at Level 33," Sterling explained. "I'm looking at you through a ultra expanded window." The elevator door slid open to reveal another door leading to the outside, with

Place 33, Secrets of Universal Truths Revealed

hundreds of tiny yellow crystals encapsulating the triangle window in the middle of it. The sunlight streamed through it in rays of gold. Then the outside door opened slowly to reveal this amazing outside dimension we were about to explore.

"Your spiritual body awaits," Sterling says with grace and love. "You can see yourself, as you are on this perfect plane."

"That's so cool!" Sherilyn says, smiling as she looks around and feels the change in frequency.

"I like looking at you," Sterling says. "Your mind is pure and your skin is flawless. You have a creamy, chiffon kind of feel. You're as healthy as mother's milk in a perfect world. You're the embodiment of purity. As we go out, you'll take your proper place inside your spiritual sphere. Take your natural place in there, and then climb within yourself."

"Okay," Sherilyn figures she'll just go with it. "I've taken my natural place and I'm within myself," Sherilyn shares. It seemed so natural, like she's done this a hundred times before, she kept thinking to herself.

"You've left the shell you walk around in while in your waking state inside the elevator. You've left your ego behind, which your body has housed for so long. You've taken up residence where you actually belong," Sterling continues.

"It's breathtaking!" she gasped with delight.

"This is 'The Place' that's appropriate for you. Here there is no taint. There is only purity. I like to see you as you are, instead of who you've become from the Life you have lived. You're a beautiful person and I'll refresh you while you're here.

We'll allow you to be who you should be, and will be going forward. We've left your tainted body behind along with your ego back in the elevator.

"Here you're finally you! Look at your hands," Sterling proclaims.

"I am! It's totally cool–like being in another world! It's like I have two separate bodies," Sherilyn says in amazement while looking at her body on the floor in the elevator.

While Sterling is staring into her beautiful blue eyes, he says, "You're sweeter than white milk chocolate. The sour smell that followed your aura around is gone. The bitterness you carried in your tongue is gone. The impurity in your blood begging to get out is no longer your reality. This is the real you as nature intended. Because there's no interference here, this is how you would've developed if your life progressed along a pure line of thought."

Sherilyn remarks, "Oh really? Tainted body? What sour smell? My tongue is bitter? Why's my blood impure? I have no clue exactly what you just said. It sounds like you're saying this is how it would be on the other side of the veil, right?"

"Yes, you will find out soon enough," Sterling says. "Let's walk down to the sea and sit on that lily pad over there."

"Sit on the lily pad?" Sherilyn remarked. In the distance she notices a beautiful, light turquoise blue sea. They begin walking toward the water's edge. It was so far away yet it seemed like they arrived so quickly.

"Okay, just put your feet in the water and let this new body fill up with the water, its an osmosis sort of thing," Sterling says. "You'll bring back the freshness and the wisdom from the knowledge of who you are in a pure and natural state to your ego body and your physical body. (The one you left in the elevator.) When you return to the physical body you live in, you'll have a memory of who you truly are."

"Wow!" Sherilyn responds.

They fill up their bodies with the water from the sea and then walk back toward the elevator. Sterling says, "Let's go back to Level 14." All of a sudden there's a *whoosh*! They are rapidly transported back to the elevator. As they walk in, Sherilyn states that she feels lighter, more pure. Slightly confused by it all, she starts to push the Ivory button for Level 14, not quite ready to get back into her physical body, but she will if she has to. They are still lying on the floor she notices.

The elevator doors open and they are outside again.

I point to a table in the park. "Look! It's a cool transparent picnic table." Sherilyn notices.

They're at a park and people are having what seems like a birthday party outside. It's a stunningly beautiful place. I notice neon-colored balloons with names on them. There's a pink sky, the sun is bright, it is very warm, and everything has a

Place 33, Secrets of Universal Truths Revealed

sunny feel to it. It is very light here, molecularly light. Everything is so light. *Sterling could easily pick up the picnic table*, I thought to myself. *In fact, I bet he can do it with one finger.*

The grass is white and I'm afraid to walk on it, worried that it might get dirty. "Wow! This is so amazing. I love the way we all look so creamy," Sherilyn recaps, with the look of astonishment on her face, while looking at Sterling's face.

Sterling says, "In this dimension we look very solid in contrast to the picnic table. Of course it's transparent; it has very few molecules. This is a Forgiven place. Everyone is forgiven here."

"Forgiven? What does that mean?" Sherilyn asks.

"Have you read the Bible?" Sterling replies.

"Yes, some of it," she answer shyly. "I went to two churches as a child. I went two or three times a week. I loved church. I went to church camp, too," Sherilyn bellows.

"Consider the birth of Christ, Mary and Joseph. What does that story correlate to?" He surveys.

"Um, maybe Christmas?" She replies, looking across the way at a pine tree she can see through.

"Birth!" Sterling blurts out. "The birth of what people should be doing now. It speaks to purity and nurturing, also known as 'Forgiven'," Sterling explains, gesturing quotation marks with his fingers.

"Forgiving what?" Sherilyn queried.

"To forgive the forces working against us, like evil and hate--you know, the opposites? Polarization is inevitable. Balancing our lives is key. The world is a blue place, which is why there is the 'Forgiven' and the 'Unforgiven.' The Unforgiven aren't to be trusted," Sterling warns.

"It's really a good place though, the Earth," Sherilyn adds with passion.

"Yes, and some will find that people are similar to vortexes of energy," Sterling remarks, "vortexes coming from the Universe gravitating towards the Earth. They're moving around inside our bodies. Depending on how old or how new we are,

we relate or don't relate to each other.
We can actually call them thoughts instead of people. "Sterling recites while looking in Sherilyn's eyes. "To truly forgive you must forget."

"Sounds like what the consciousness of Abraham always says, "Get in the vortex." "Is everyone capable of forgiveness, being forgiven?" Sherilyn questions him.

"Definitely! There's a preference of who should be with whom," he says. "Because we're all better off with our enlightened match. Either you're a Forgiven or an Unforgiven soul. Most of us work through many, many people before finding the person who best suits us and makes us whole in a reciprocal manner. As far as wanting a soul mate, always look to the left Sherilyn," Sterling states.

"Ok, that sounds like law of attraction," Sherilyn interjects. "Am I a good match for Kenton? I kind of like him. I just met him, but I feel like we have a connection," Sherilyn says.

"You're a very good match for Kenton. He's the kind of guy who understands the value of feminine energy. Kenton's a more progressed male. There aren't many. They're hard to find. Most men are afraid of female energy. Sterling chuckles.

"However the new feminine energy and power is on the horizon. Only a few, select men have the ability and insight to progress to a level where they can handle the transitory period of change we're in right now," Sterling articulates.

"What do you mean?" Sherilyn asks, not quite understanding how energy works.

"We're changing from a society focused on masculine energy into one focused on feminine energy. It started changing after Dec 21, 2012 and it's a good thing. We needed to discover how to allow the juxtaposition of energy to flow. But you're also misplaced," he added.

"Why am I misplaced? I'm confused," Sherilyn asks quizzically.

"Because you weren't born with, nor did you come by (gain) the kind of enlightenment needed to protect and shield yourself from Unforgiven souls. Unforgiven people haven't learned to forgive. They're not bad. They're simply on the

Place 33, Secrets of Universal Truths Revealed

other side of forgiveness. They live in the shadow of themselves. The primary objective of your misplacement is that it was contrived. You're pristine as a being. The begotten daughter of Angie," Sterling says, smiling.

"What? Contrived? Who is Angie? How do you know this stuff about me?" Sherilyn looks bewildered.

Sterling goes on to say, "Here in the Elevator of Enlightenment all secrets are revealed. You see there are always two sides due to polarization. You haven't gone to the other side of The Place yet, right?" he asks, knowing the real truth.

"No, remember, this is my first time in the elevator," Sherilyn reminds him.

"I know you've been there before," Sterling says. "You just don't remember. It's somewhat like a rabbit hole. We'll have to go there on a field trip sometime.

On the other side of The Place there is damp, stinky, rotting elevator you must take to get there. That's where the Unforgiven souls are hanging out. They have to become saturated with negativity before ever shifting to the Forgiven side. Most don't know of this elevator."

"It seems counter-intuitive," Sterling states. "When they fully saturate themselves with negativity to a degree, they actually transcend and rise above it."

"How do you do that, become Forgiven?" Sherilyn asks.

He replies, "You get there only by gaining the wisdom of clarity--by forgiving everyone and everything that's ever happened to you and most of all forgive yourself."

"Oh," Sherilyn replies in a state of confusion. "That's almost impossible." looking back on her life.

As they are talking about Forgiven and Unforgiven souls, Sherilyn is catching balloons floating in the air. She finds a balloon with her name on it. She starts tying the balloons to the trees. You can actually see through the trees. We are sitting at a picnic table. Sterling is looking into the picnic table, which looks like some sort of Ultra-Dimensional Map.

Sterling starts explaining, "Okay, we're at the 'City of Movement Ultra Map.' I can see the presence in your hotel room you were talking about when we met in the elevator. She's hanging out there in the bathroom."

"Yeah, that's where I heard tapping on the bathroom pipes," Sherilyn replies.

"She's stuck! She has emotions attached to the event of her death. She isn't back in a body again because her composite is incomplete. She's stuck! Part of her is stuck because she won't let go of her thoughts about that life. Occasionally this happens, but it's rare. Her emotions are involved in her thoughts. She's stuck to the matter within the dimensions that make up your room."

"What?" Sherilyn screams. "The matter that makes up the room? Can you help her? It would be wonderful if you could, so she can leave. My kids are going to see her and jump into my bed in the middle of the night."

"You'll always hear noises there because she's extremely unhappy," Sterling educates Sherilyn.

"Yes," Sherilyn replies. "I hear creaks from doors, movement and tapping."

Sterling is not surprised because it's energy outside the perimeter. The perimeter is another dimension and the energy of her soul is trying to get out.

"Is she a Forgiven soul" Sherilyn asks.

"I don't know. I'd have to ask," Sterling replied.

"Ask, please, whoever you have to ask. Just help me get her out of our room!" Sherilyn says with fear in her voice.

"Okay, let's go back to the elevator. We need to go to a different Level first." Sterling coaxes.

Sherilyn follows Sterling back to the Elevator of Enlightenment, trying to grasp this around her mind.

Sterling says, "The mind has trouble letting go sometimes. Let's get in the elevator and go to Level 33." Almost like magic, we are *whooshed* to Level 33 again. As the elevator doors open, we enter a beautiful place with healing green energy. Beautiful tall trees all seem to be crying like they are alive, like in the wizard of Oz.

"We're in the crying place now," Sterling says. We have to go through it to get to the Place, 'Place 33.'"

Place 33, Secrets of Universal Truths Revealed

"Why are the trees crying?" Sherilyn asks.

"You must understand the lesson. It's the lesson of the tear. Sherilyn is crying which makes the trees cry. She took on too much and now she's confused," he says.

"Why must I learn that lesson?" Sherilyn probed.

"It's a hard one, I know," Sterling admits.

"Was I supposed to do that? Take on so much?" Sherilyn queried.

"Probably not, but you chose to anyway. We always have choice. Let's leave The Crying Place for now. This is a cousin of Place 33," says Sterling. We continue walking down a path and finally reach the shores of an amazing, still White Sea. It's very clear, like a sea of light.

"It is so bright in here; God, it's an amazing place. Even though I've been here so many times, it never fails to amaze me. I love coming here." Sterling smiles while he's explaining the other side.

"When do you usually come here, when you sleep?" Sherilyn asks. "I'm sure I've dreamt of this place," she whispers to herself.

"Gee, I don't know. You've been here in the Afterlife," Sterling explains. "its so amazing, so pure white. I love it! It smells so pure. There's a huge green lily pad over there we can sit on. It's fanciful but it's a real place. It's to the left in the left hemisphere, a huge place. I always know how to come here." Sterling says smiling.

Sherilyn sits with Sterling on the lily pad and asks, "How do I look?"

"Well, you're smiling so big" Sterling says.

Sherilyn looks at him with deep warmth and says, "I don't know why, but I love you!"

"I love you, too," Sterling says. "The Love Vibration is always strong here. Here you are truly in love." There is this pink mist like substance all around us.

"Are you happy?" She asks him.

"Why, yes!" he replies. Then, as if noticing her face for the first time, he adds, "You have such creamy skin." His eyes lock with hers as he gazes. "Oh my God! We are being transported to another place, outside of time and space," Sterling shouts.

The Visitation

By Sherilyn B. Avalon

Chapter 5 - The Visitation

Startled Sherilyn asks, "Where are we?" getting caught up in the cosmic love vibration that they were just transcended into.

Amazing flowers surround us. "I can hear their voices and they sound so beautiful, so lovely," Sherilyn responds. "It's glorious, so crystal white. Everything has a white sheen with many crystals of beautiful colors of pinks, blues, and violet, as they surround us."

"I love the sounds here; it's heavenly," Sterling says. "The sky is a magnificent emerald green. Everything is white but the sky is green. I'm the same color as the white light around us and you have such creamy skin," Sterling keeps staring at Sherilyn.

Sherilyn laughs like a little girl. "Yeah I see that. But what are we doing here?"

"We're playing, playing with the flowers," he answered.

Still caught up in the Divine Cosmic Love Vibration Sherilyn asks, "Can you answer some questions?"

"Sure" he says, as the sky is growing darker.

"What does the future hold for me? Do you know?" Sherilyn thought he might know.

"Love, we all must love each other. I love you. When you're here, everyone is filled with Divine Cosmic Love. Everyone experiences an intense, unconditional love for one another," Sterling says while emanating Divine Love.

"Do you see anyone here? Like maybe our guardian angels? Do you have a guardian angel? Do I have one? I thought I would ask because I have heard some people have guides and angels," Sherilyn responds. "I had this dream about my guardian angel."

"Yes, and she loves you," he says, chuckling softly. "Her name is Angie. She used to be a Man. She is both Male and Female energy."

"Mother/Father God, maybe?" Sherilyn asks perplexed. She burst out laughing repeating her name. "Angie, right?

Angie. Yes it feels right. What's your guardian angel's name?" Sherilyn asks Sterling.

"Frank," Sterling retorts into bursts of laughter, also.

"Frank! What do you think about Frank?" Sherilyn probes.

"He likes me. He thinks I'm funny," Sterling answers.

"Do they help us? What do they say about us?" Sherilyn asks. Sherilyn has so many questions to ask.

"Angie loves you. You're going to be okay," Sterling states, then he's starting to cry.

"I'm okay, I think," Sherilyn said. Then she starts reflecting on her life so far. "Yes, it has been hard. But I believe I needed to learn some of that stuff to overcome it," Sherilyn declared in that state of mind.

"Look! Empty chairs in the field over there," Sterling said, pointing toward the chairs in this field of gold, that looks like wheat, next to the vibrant shining flowers. "They're about to be filled with souls," Sterling exclaimed. We run over to them. Sterling and I are holding hands. We are watching for anyone, mainly the ones who are supposed to be seated in the chairs.

"Can we sit in the chairs?" Sherilyn questioned.

"No, we're not supposed to sit down yet," Sterling replied.

"Oh, okay," Sherilyn, says, noticing the grass is starting to turn brilliantly vibrant green beyond the golden wheat. "Will there be a wedding? Looks like a set up for a wedding."

"Mmm-mmm. I don't think so," he says. "It looks like a Visitation. It's very nice here. There's no reason to be afraid of anything," Sterling declared.

"Look! The sky's turning this fascinating cobalt blue. Where are we?" Sherilyn asks.

"This is 'The Place, Place 33' but, a different part of The Place." Sterling voices.

"What part is this?" She asked.

"It is to the right," he replied. "You're just going a different way with me. It's okay with me."

Sherilyn thinks for a moment about her life that was filled with much pain, before stepping into the Elevator of Enlightenment in the basement of Vegas Indoor Skydiving.

Place 33, Secrets of Universal Truths Revealed

She remembered she needed to get back to the advertisement she's designing, and the entity in her hotel room, Room 333. "I'm getting a little impatient," Sherilyn retorts.

"The air smells fresh and clean, like honey and pine. It's delightful here. I don't want to leave, but, I need to get back," Sherilyn stated.

"They're coming. We're waiting," Sterling verbalizes. "Smell that, take a deep breath. I've turned green! It feels good, I just soaked up the green energy," he says.

"Cool! Color modeling. What color am I now?" Sherilyn asked.

"You're white! Wait, now you're gradually turning green. You're pure here and protected. But, you shouldn't go by yourself quite yet," he says. "No, you're an innocent person, like a child. You go too quickly."

"Are they coming?" Sherilyn inquired.

"They're getting closer," he says. Then, Sterling quickly changes the subject. "You look so beautiful. Your eyes are blue. I can feel your purity here. Angie is coming. She's watching you. She spreads her dazzling robe, and it's like raining sunshine. She's the most nurturing person I've ever seen or felt. She gives me goose bumps everywhere. I can feel her now! Can you feel her? She's there. I see her in the sky, waiting. She loves you like a child, Sherilyn."

"What? Why?" Sherilyn asks excitedly because she gets to finally meet her guardian Angel.

"Come sit down, Frank. He's grumbling again because he never wants to do anything. He thinks it's all so stupid. He thinks it's a hassle," mutters Sterling under his breath.

"What's stupid?" Sherilyn questioned. She can tell Frank frightens Sterling.

"What we have to do, to learn," he answers.

"Frank thinks learning is stupid?" She queried.

"Well, he knows it's not. That's right, just hold my hand, it's okay. I see Angie, and she's waiting on Frank again. Frank's always late," Sterling uttered.

Suddenly there's a noisy rustling sound and Frank pops up right before Sterling's face. Sterling says, "Whoa!" "He can be kind of scary sometimes. Actually he can just be an asshole. He's a trickster," stated Sterling.

"Your Guardian Angel is a trickster?" Sherilyn asked Sterling sweetly.

Sterling says, "Come on Frank sit down, we're all waiting for you." In the same breath with a booming laugh toward Frank he says, "Okay, I know, okay. By the way Sherilyn, Angie is smiling."

Sherilyn asks, "Is she? What did Frank say?"

Place 33, Secrets of Universal Truths Revealed

Then Sterling introduces her. "Frank, meet Sherilyn. Sherilyn this is Frank." Out of the blue Sterling says, "Isn't he an ugly bastard?"

Sherilyn gasped. "I thought he was your Guardian Angel? How could you say that? That's no way to talk to your Guardian Angel, is it?"

He wasn't ugly at all. He was Beautiful! All things are beautiful on the other side and...naked.

"What's going on Frank?" Sterling inquired. "Glad you could make it. You don't like sitting down, do ya? Ha-ha-ha, I'm glad finally someone made you do something, Frank's okay, but he could be better," he says chuckling again.

"This sure is odd. Is he coming back to Earth?" Sherilyn questioned.

"No. Oh no, he doesn't have to. I don't know if Angie will sit down or not. Frank's sitting., he has brown skin, long brown hair, and he walks around naked everywhere. He never puts on clothes, ever," he says.

Sherilyn wonders if perhaps he's originally from India or American Indian. "He kind of looks like Jesus," she ponders.

"Yet..." Sterling heard her. "Yeah, you might say so and yet... "Well, ask him."

"Okay"... Sherilyn blurts out... "Frank, are you Jesus?" Turning back to her Sterling confides, "He gave you the finger!"

"What?" Sherilyn now embarrassed.

"He thinks you're funny. Yeah, Frank thinks everybody's funny but him. But, Frank always comes through in the end," Sterling adds.

Sherilyn is a bit stunned; then she finds herself hysterical with laughter. "That's some great angel, huh? What about Angie, is she coming down?" She asked.

"She's been hovering above us the entire time. She is so gorgeous. It is tough for her to sit down," Sterling says, "because sitting just isn't something she does. She will though. Do you see her?"

Sherilyn turned around. "Yes! Oh my God. Yes, I see her now! Wow, she takes up almost the whole sky."

"Yeah, she's beautiful at 42." (Sterling reveals why he knows her age later to Sherilyn). "Will you sit down Angie? Sit down, and be your old self for a little while. Sherilyn needs to talk to you now." Sterling turns to Sherilyn and adds, "She says okay."

"Thank you Angie, thank you," Sherilyn utters while staring at her amazing beauty.

"It's a privilege just to look at her. She shimmers. You can see right through her. She's not capable of looking like flesh," he says, "You're incredibly fortunate to have her. Would you like to ask Angie a question? She is sitting there on the chair now." Sterling verbalizes.

"Yeah, I would like to ask her, what should I do about my four children and my ex-boyfriend?" Sherilyn stated.

Sterling says, "She likes our color green, she approves of it."

Reluctantly Sherilyn questioned, "She's a nice Guardian Angel, right?"

"She is as nice as anyone can be. I love her," Sterling replied. She's saying, 'Hold my hand.' If you hold her hand you'll be protected."

"How do I do that?" Sherilyn asks, afraid to touch Angie, her so called Guardian Angel.

"Just do it!" Sterling instructs. "She'll extend her hand to you. She has a loving energy. She's different, powerful and she'll help you with what you want to do. Isn't that right Angie?"

Telepathically, Angie replies with a soft, "Yes."

Sherilyn shyly says, "Tell her thank you for me."

"You tell her," Sterling answered.

"Sherilyn is a young person and an old person." "She's young in this lifetime, but she's an old soul," Angie relays.

"Angie loves you very much. You weren't supposed to be so severely hurt this time."

"Then why did I get so hurt?" Sherilyn asked, intensely curious.

Place 33, Secrets of Universal Truths Revealed

Angie replies through Sterling: "Nothing is perfect in its perfection. That's something even some enlightened people don't always understand."

"I just read Angie. She doesn't speak, because she doesn't need to express that way," Sterling explained. "It's perfectly clear what's in her mind. If she wants to allow you to see it, she will. She is the clearest of the Angels. She'll love your children but we all must take responsibility for our actions," Angie explained.

"Why doesn't she look like flesh?" Sherilyn asks, confused. "I guess she is just too far removed, detached from human flesh. She is so pure — pure energy, almost. She probably still has a few molecules left so you can see her but not very many. She's more of a presence." Highly intense, Sterling informed her. "She's almost pure love. She is an exalted spirit, and she's watching over you because you're somewhat misplaced."

"Yeah, you said that to me before. Why am I misplaced?" She asked.

He responds, "You weren't supposed to go through so much pain this time. That's why she pays special attention to you. It was like a mistake, so now she has an extraordinary interest in you. I'm reading her thoughts now. Angie is sorry, but it wasn't her fault. She had nothing to do with it. She's protecting you as long as you believe; she'll create a clear path for you. You can have a miracle. We all have a strong focus on you because you're misplaced."

"Really? I can have a miracle?" Sherilyn verbalizes.

"Yes!" replies Sterling. He paused, as he stared intently at Angie. "It's just outstanding being in her presence. She's sitting there now, not going anywhere. She's comfortable with it now, and knows she did the right thing. Touch her Sherilyn! Touch her!"

"Touch Angie?" Sherilyn repeats.

"Yes, reach out to her! Touch her…touch her! You're afraid, Sherilyn. Why are you afraid?"

"Help me, Sterling. Tell me how to be more courageous," Sherilyn implored.

"Touch her, sweetie!" Sterling says gently. "She's reaching

out. It's okay. Touch her and you'll be protected. Get closer to her, touch her. You take so long to do everything!"

"I'm very cautious. I'm new at this," she states.

Finally, through Sherilyn's intention, somehow she touches Angie.

Sterling laughs, "Good, I'm glad! You're dancing with her! You're inside her, and the two of you are dancing. You're dancing on the lawn."

Yes, Sherilyn noticed they were dancing. It was amazing. She was dancing inside this magnificent light being. It was as if they were melding and floating together.

"I was becoming one with the entire Universe. My molecules were changing. I felt every cell of my being was regenerating as my mind was renewing. It reminds me of what Jesus said in the Bible. 'Be ye renewed by the renewing of your mind.'" Sherilyn wept.

Then Sterling says, "That's good, stay inside her. Mmm-hmm. Just soak her up."

Sherilyn felt sad she started thinking of her children, her family. Her whole life flashed before her. She got lost in the thoughts of golden beaches and gently swaying palm trees.

Sterling says, "I'm glad she let you in. You're very fortunate. You deserve it, Sherilyn."

"I feel so much better. It was so weird; so weird, that I'm still in shock. For the first time, I was literally filled with light," Sherilyn whispers.

"Yes, you're going to be okay now. There's no way you won't be okay now. It wasn't supposed to happen like this. You'll finally get all the good you deserve; everyone does in the end. It's good that you did this!" Sterling says.

"Thank you Angie, I love you," she blurts out.

"Frank wants to talk to you Sherilyn," Sterling says.

"Frank is saying, 'Okay, that's enough! Let her out, let her go. That is enough. You got it! Let her go now.' Yet I can tell you don't want to let go. She's beautiful isn't she?" Sterling says, "I love her."

"How do I look now?" Sherilyn asks Sterling. She was caught up in the spirit of the moment.

Place 33, Secrets of Universal Truths Revealed

Sherilyn after transformation with Angie

"Oh you're glowing, sweetie. You're practically on fire! You're very lucky. There's always two sides, just remember that," Sterling says.

Graciously Sherilyn says, "Thank you Angie and Frank, and Sterling!"

"Frank doesn't want to go either," says Sterling.

"Oh, all right," Frank, lamented. But you look so gorgeous filled with light, that I simply can't contain my self." He left Sherilyn to saturate with the light, and when she was through, he left.

"Does he have work to do?" Sherilyn asks.

"Of a kind," Sterling replies. "He has the power to interfere. Frank has no title. He's known by what he does."

"What does he do?" She asks.

"Frank is like the wind. He's like a gale of control to make things go one-way or the other," Sterling reveals.

"He has the ability to do that? Is he God?" She wonders aloud.

Sterling reveals, "He used to be. *He's a Tester*, which is an important position. It's not referred to as anything specific, it's just done. He watches, listens, he feels, he learns and he helps."

"I guess the best 'title' would be to call him 'The Interferer'," Sterling replies. "He helps begrudgingly. He sits crouched and he grumbles a lot. He actually teaches through Pain. Pain is a good thing. At least to Frank, pain is a good thing; because he thinks you learn more with pain, and more quickly that way. He helps because he wants us to move on."

"But how does he help?" Sherilyn asks.

"He helps with the enlightenment of people who call upon him, who he has in his files," Sterling interposes.

"Files? How many does he have?" Sherilyn responds.

"I guess that's part of the intrigue. Hundreds!" Sterling says with respect. "I don't know how many Angie helps. I can't put a number on it," Sterling says. "Some people would call her an Angel, but she doesn't call herself that."

"No, why not?" asks Sherilyn.

"Because she's pure consciousness! He answers. "She and Frank have no reason to be verbal. There is no point to it. We on Earth have a more limited consciousness. We have a need, a desire to understand things and they don't need that. They're more free-flowing."

"I'm sending God's Love to Frank. Does he feel it?" asks Sherilyn with a smile. She new it would melt his heart.

"Oh yeah, he's a part of God, Sherilyn. He definitely has a lot more molecules than Angie. He doesn't ever have to come back though. Don't worry about that. We're the ones in trouble," Sterling informs her.

"So we have to come back all the time?" Sherilyn exclaims. "Never in a million years would I have ever dreamed this could happen to me. Now I get it. Reincarnation is real!"

"You don't always have to come back," Sterling stuttered. "Frank knows after I die on Earth I'll be his boss! I'm not really

Place 33, Secrets of Universal Truths Revealed

supposed to be here. Here being the operative word," replies Sterling.

"I thought you were the janitor of the Indoor Skydiving place," Sherilyn exclaims.

"Well, Frank is a trickster and so am I," says Sterling. "You'll pay for this Frank!" In addition, Sterling was on the verge of panic, looking down to the right *because, Frank is always crouched down looking on man from there at Place 33.* "He tricked me into coming back here; He actually tricked us both!"

"I'm mystified that something so unbelievable could have occurred. Let me get this right, you're taking over his position? Where is 'back here?' You mean back on Earth?" Sherilyn asks.

"Yes, this world!" Sterling replies with discontent. "It's okay he'll pay, he knows, don't you Frank?" Sterling says with wry laughter. "He's worried I'll treat him like he's treated me." Frank is frantically pacing back and forth.

It startled Sherilyn to hear this. "Uh oh, is that Karma?" She quizzes him.

"Well, Karma is the Law. It became the Law through Polarization." he replied.

"So you'll be Frank's boss? But, he won't be on Earth, right?" she inquires.

"Oh no, he's not there now. He hasn't been on Earth in a long time," he says.

"So beyond the veil you're the boss?" Asks Sherilyn, rephrasing the question.

"Yes, I'll take over Frank's position," says Sterling. "It doesn't categorically have a name though."

"Right! How do you take over that position?" Sherilyn asked.

"I am next!" Sterling replied. "I've lived long enough to be there, and, I've made enough correct decisions for the soul, or the conscious entity that lines up for this position. They always are of their own character, or something a little different," he says. He's wondering if he should have mentioned that to Sherilyn now. It was against his better judgment.

"Will you have a temper?" Sherilyn asked in a condescending tone like she was speaking to an unruly child.

"Somewhat, though I won't interfere like Frank does. I'll help people and reward them with pleasure. I'll teach them that way rather than punishing them and making them learn the hard way. Angie and I will work together. It'll be better that way. We can't let Kenton know of this," Sterling pleads.

"That sounds good!" She says...thinking yeah, he's nuts!

"Frank's capable of that, but it isn't his style. Angie finds his style irritating. She doesn't like it even though she knows it works.

She doesn't play games; she simply showers people with the wisdom of love. She's very magnetic for them. *When you're in touch with her presence you do this, too, Sherilyn,*" Sterling claimed.

She took a deep breath and says, "Yes, I guess so, when I connect with her energy like I just did. Do they see us from where they are, or do they have to go closer to Earth to see us?"

"Well, they're always with us; but, we need to tap into their energy so we can communicate with them. You can tap in through the Elevator of Enlightenment, through meditation, or through prayer," he said.

Sherilyn was always told prayer is the way to communicate with God and the Angels. "You can communicate through hypnosis, meditation, sometimes a near-death experience, or even some drugs. Whatever actually *warps the parameter of your mind* on Earth," explained Sterling.

Sherilyn raised her eyebrows. "So I'm saved now? That was my miracle?"

"You're a beautiful person. You were misplaced and Angie took care of it. It was all her, and it was at the expense of some others. So you better come through! You're much more powerful than you think. You're the one who is now exposed to different levels and dimensions. You were going to have a horrible life!" Sterling exclaimed.

Sherilyn now realized they changed her life frequency. Her thoughts grew clearer. She felt more love and compassion for everyone and everything. She came from a depressed, guilt-ridden emotional state and place due to her children and her exe's. Growing up in a dysfunctional family environment didn't help.

Sherilyn smiled and reached for Sterling's hand. "Don't worry about it," she says. "You've done an incredible job getting me this far. I thought for sure, I'd be on the streets next week. Thank you for all your help. Angie I love you," she said. Then turning to Sterling asks, "Will we come back here again?"

"Oh yes, now you can leave your body in the world and come to The Place and travel around to all the dimensions through hypnosis. You're infinitely eight." *(You'll find out what that means later.)*

"We need to get back to the Elevator of Enlightenment, though. Let's go back to 3D Earth," suggested Sterling.

Instantly we were back to Earth in the Elevator of Enlightenment. Our Physical bodies were sleeping on the floor. We slipped back into them. The doors to the elevator opened again to the familiar basement at Vegas Indoor Skydiving.

"Wow! The whole thing is so unreal. It's almost too much to believe. I need to go home and pick up my babies. Thank you, Angie. Thank you, Frank. I love you!" Sherilyn said.

As we get ready to walk back toward the lobby. Sherilyn picked up her purse, and immediately saw Tony. He was cleaning the filters down the hall. She hoped he didn't see her. Sherilyn said her goodbyes to Sterling and thanked him for his help.

Sterling reminds Sherilyn, "Before we go I want to tell you about Kenton. Remember, Kenton is the kind of guy who understands the value of Female Energy. He'll help you with a lot of things. But I'm the one who can help you go to the different levels and explore them. I am to be with you for 33 weeks, and you'll fall in love again. However, first we must change your energy."

"Really? Okay," she says, excitedly. Of course, it is certainly possible that had Angie, St. Stephan and Frank not supervened at this time who knows where I would be.

As we are talking and walking up the stairs Sterling turns to Sherilyn and says, "If you'd like to know more about God or Source, let me know. Maybe we can learn together." Then he turned and walked down the hall and disappeared.

Sherilyn kept walking toward the front desk and ran into Kenton.

Handsome Kenton says, "Hi sweetie, I just got out of a meeting. I was wondering if you got that advertisement finished."

"Why yes darling, I do," Sherilyn replied with a wink. She pulled it out of her purse and handed it to him. "What do you think?" She asked.

He looked it over for a moment and says, "It's absolutely perfect; exactly what I wanted."

"Awesome," she responded.

Then he says, "By the way you look beautiful today. I didn't know you had blue eyes. Your eyes are positively glowing!"

Sherilyn replied, "Thank you, sometimes they're blue, and, sometimes they're green. It depends on what I wear that day."

Kenton says, "Let me write you a check."

They walk over to his office. He glances at the clock. "Do you want to have lunch together?"

"I'm sorry, how about tomorrow? I'm super-busy today," she replies hopefully.

"Okay, then. How 'bout noon, tomorrow?" Kenton asks, smiling at her with those luscious lips.

"Sure thing," she says. "I'll meet you here. Thank you." He hands her the check, then she drives off to pick up her little girls.

Place 33, Secrets of Universal Truths Revealed

The advertisement I made

Chapter 6 - First Momentum

The day was blustery and bleak. The wind blew fast and hard, whistling through the windows making eerie sounds. Debris like plastic bags and feathers from a pigeon's nest flew by. Mulberry tops littered the porch of the hotel room.

"A storm is brewing," Sherilyn says out loud to herself. A little dust devil pops up! It reminds her of the wind tunnel. "Time to get ready for a lunch date with Kenton," she says to herself.

Sherilyn dropped Margot and Sally off at school already. She's wondering if she should tell Kenton she has children yet. Or, if She should tell him how many children She has? "Oh well, I'll just play it by ear." She talks to her self while driving on the way to the tunnel.

Sherilyn pulls up to the door and he's waiting for her. She rolls down the window and says, "Hi!" She's embarrassed because she drives old silver, 1990 Nissan Truck that needs a paint job. "Starving artist," she says, while shrugging her shoulders.

"I see we both like trucks," he says. Except his is a big, brand new Ford F150 4x4.

"Let's go in mine," he shouts through the window.

"Yeah, okay. I'll park the beast," Sherilyn replied.

"Where do you want to go? Sushi?" he asked.

"Yes, let's," she says with a sunny grin. As he opened the door for her to climb inside, he apologized for the truck being so dirty. "No problem," she replied. The list of questions she wanted to ask him suddenly became blurred. Obviously, Kenton was having a hypnotic effect on her.

They eat and talk about the Elevator of Enlightenment. He says, "We'll go check it out after lunch."

Sherilyn says, "Cool! I'm so excited."

They finish lunch and return to the Wind Tunnel. "Okay, let's go to the elevator," Kenton says. Kenton enters the code and the doors open. To their surprise Sterling is inside.

"Hi Sterling," Kenton says. "Meet Sherilyn."

Place 33, Secrets of Universal Truths Revealed

Sherilyn says, "Oh, we've met!" Kenton looks a little perplexed.

"Yesterday--we met when you were in your meeting--while I waited," she explained.

Kenton gets a text on his cell phone again. "Damn, I got to take this. Sterling, would you take Sherilyn for a ride? I promised her a ride in the elevator."

"Sure thing!" Sterling replied.

Kenton looks at Sherilyn with puppy dog eyes and says, "I'm sorry, sweetie. We'll talk when you get back, okay?" Kenton winks.

"Yeah, sounds good!" she answers him. So off to the elevator they go again.

"Whew! That was awkward. I didn't tell Kenton about our trip the other day." Sherilyn informed Sterling.

"You're not obligated to tell anyone, are you?" Sterling teases her. "I don't know where you want to go today. The elevator will take us anywhere. For lessons unlearned go to Level 33." He then pauses and says, "Have you thought about what I mentioned yesterday?"

"Yes, I did. I'd like to know more about God's energy. I'd like to know more about God, some call him Source or even Holy Spirit." Then she added, "Do you know that presence, the entity, is still in my room? It was tapping on the pipes again."

"Okay, I know exactly where to go. I haven't been there in a long time, but I'm sure it'll be intriguing. Are you ready?" Sterling asked.

"Yes," Sherilyn replies. They step in the Elevator of Enlightenment. Whoosh, they are off again.

They stop quickly so Sherilyn asks, "Where are we?"

On Level 12 there's a dark hole with a light on top. All of a sudden a window opens up.

We're looking out the window. "Can we go to The Place?" Sherilyn questioned.

"No, not today," Sterling replies. "We're on the other side of The Place today." Sterling appears startled as he looks out the window. "There are painful bodies here. This is a place of painful bodies."

"Painful bodies!" Sherilyn replied.

"I can see my pain. It looks as if the trees are on fire. These red trees almost make me hurt. They need to be put out like flames," Sterling recites.

"Can you do that?" Sherilyn asks Sterling as she stares at the trees that are on fire with bodies in them.

"God can do it."

"Can you ask God to help you?"

"Angie's here, but I'm stubborn," Sterling replied. "I don't want to ask God. God's watching me and he wants to know what I'm going to do next."

"Did God say that?" Sherilyn asked.

"That's what Frank said. I can hear him. I hear Angie, too. She's watching along with Frank. They know I'm on the other side. The trees make my arm hurt." Sterling relayed.

"If you're hurting, ask God to help you, Sterling. Ask him," Sherilyn implores.

"Too big!" he blurts out.

"What's too big? You're too big?" She asked.

"I'm not quite ready to ask," he said.

"Okay," Sherilyn murmurs.

"That's why I'm being punished. I can take a lot. Come with me, let's float up," Sterling said.

They walk down a path and slip inside these big, light green to clear colored bubbles. They left their physical bodies in the elevator again. They are shifting into another dimension. Their spiritual bodies change shape and energy and form to these balloon type bubbles. As they float upward, Sherilyn is asking Sterling questions.

"Who is God?" Sherilyn asked, figuring it makes sense to start from the beginning.

"He's energy that's left the flesh," Sterling answered. "He started with momentum. He was the first momentum."

"It's that easy? Why do we call God 'he'? He doesn't have a gender does he?" she asked.

"He does to me," Sterling relayed.

"Why?" Sherilyn probed.

Place 33, Secrets of Universal Truths Revealed

"Because that's how he feels, like a father," Sterling says with conviction.

"Are we going up?" She said.

"Can we just stare at the magnificent beauty of the wall for a minute?" Sterling said.

They are scaling the wall now. "It's never going to end, is it?" Sherilyn examines.

They look on in amazement at the enormity of the wall that is what some call God or Source.

"We know him as 'father' in the Bible. What does that mean?" Sherilyn tests.

"It means he's a beloved spirit. He's larger than everything. He has no limitations or boundaries. I don't know much about God. I just see him. It's very clear to me," Sterling explained

"That's the energy of God or what some call Source?" Sherilyn inquired. She can't believe she is looking at God.

"Mmm-hmmm. It's like a big, never-ending wall. It goes on and on; it's just pure, alive energy," Sterling Stated.

"Yeah, while we're floating." Sherilyn noticed something's different. "Are we in him?" She asked.

"We're in two big, pale green balloons. They're kind of like bubbles. Sterling replied. I'm not sure why, but it feels good; we're protected inside these spheres. We've been rising for a long time. It's like being on a ride. The wall of God is so thick, so long. We're experiencing just a very insignificant piece," Sterling replied.

"Why do some people call God, Jehovah?" Sherilyn probes.

"People are highly subjective. There are many names for God: He, Yahweh, Jehovah, Source; some call God, Allah.

It doesn't really matter. *God is all encompassing, pure energy with benevolent feelings*. The principles set forth can't be manipulated. That simply won't work. No, the energy must be understood as a flowing thing," Sterling replies.

"Like a faucet or a river?" Sherilyn questioned. This reminds her of the book about Edgar Cayce, "There is a river, by Thomas Sugrue" Maybe that's what he was talking about. The river.

"Yeah, it flows," Sterling says. It's like learning to use a rope with a lasso like a cowboy. It is fluid and it ebbs and flows."

"Fluid energy? Does it go through your vortex, your Chakras?" Sherilyn reviews.

"Yeah," he said.

"How do you ask for it? Just pray?" She asked.

"Yeah, you can do that." Sterling replied.

"Do you have to pray to Jesus to reach God?" Sherilyn questioned.

"No! People say that because they're subjective," he replied.

"What about our Guardian Angels? Do you pray through your Angels to get to God?" She asked.

"It easier for some people that way, because it's in their belief system. It's true for many. But everyone doesn't have to do it that way," Sterling says.

"Do I?" Sherilyn questioned.

He replies, "Yes, for now you do. But that's subject to change, when you change your belief system."

"Oh, do you?" Sherilyn asked.

"No," Sterling replied.

"How come I do?" Sherilyn asks a little upset.

"Ask God," he says.

Gazing skyward to the magnificent energy, Sherilyn asked, "God, why must I go through my guardian angel to reach you?"

God speaks to her and is saying, "Because you're a benevolent, you have the innocence to the degree of one-third."

"Only one-third?" She replied.

"That's what's left right now. You can't just be there, Sherilyn. Right now, it would cloud your understanding. You need a little help. Innocence is bliss, but bliss is also ignorance. That's how it works," God relayed telepathically.

Place 33, Secrets of Universal Truths Revealed

"So ignorance is bliss, right? Will I be able to understand in this lifetime?" Sherilyn inquired.

"Almost-- you could make it," he relayed.

"I certainly hope so. Then I won't have to come back? I can go to The Place and stay there all the time." Sherilyn wishes.

"That's right. It's where we all want to be. Then it all becomes clear. You'll be part of it, and you'll be there with the rest. That's when we'll fulfill our purpose," God telepathically relayed.

"And our 'purpose' is?" Sherilyn asked.

"Moving on," Sterling simply said.

"What do I have to do to get there?" Sherilyn implored.

"You must get rid of your one-third by asking God," Sterling declared.

"Do I constantly have to keep asking God?" Sherilyn asked Sterling.

"Angie always smiles when you ask," Sterling says lovingly.

"Does she?"

"Angie smiles because she loves you. You try hard and sometimes you backslide. Temptation gets to you," Sterling informs her.

"What? What do I backslide on?"

"The Truth, which is Self-Centeredness." He replied.

"Oh I see, yeah. Can we go to 'The Place', Place 33 today? ...One more time?" She pleads.

Sterling replied, "The Place is all around us today. Well, it's like the energy of The Place is present with God. Yeah, it's the woven fabric of energy from The Place. To actually be there is truly exceptional."

"I know, I love it there. Would you say it's like waves?"

"It's actually interwoven," Sterling says. "Here it comes right from God. It's almost like a matrix, but it's entwined. It's like ribbons. It's complicated, but also incredibly simple because that's how polarization works. Everything is a mirror image of itself."

"Where is the other part?" Sherilyn asked.

"It is always there. You must look to the left, always look to the left. The right is more concrete." Sterling stops and says, "Oooh! Do you see it? On the left you'll discover the Blessing." Angie's smiling big.

"Is it an illusion? Sherilyn queried him.

"Oh, no it's quite real! On the right is the stuff we use to put in a bottle. A frame," he explains.

"What's that?" Sherilyn examines.

"Parameters or limitations are the selfish needs people have, because we lack the open-minded view to simply let the left take over." Sterling says with enthusiasm.

"I always say we don't need limits," Sherilyn announces, puffing up like a parrot.

"But you do, because without parameters you'd be in The Place," Sterling retorts.

"Ohhh! Can you go to The Place if you meditate?" Sherilyn asked

"You can get close. Unfortunately for many people, they think they actually have to die," Sterling says plainly.

"Not all people?" Sherilyn reacts inquisitively.

"Some of us are more dead than others. That's because the more lives you've lived, the closer to dead you are." Sterling smiles.

"Are you referring to past lives?" Sherilyn asked inquisitively.

"People call it dead, it's really more alive. It's the mirror image, you know."

"Yeah, I like that." Sherilyn smiles. "Okay, How many lifetimes do you have to experience before you can be with God at the Place?"

"Many lives. Hundreds of lives! Too many," says Sterling.

"Too many, really? Why must we be on Earth?" Sherilyn asked.

"Being on Earth is important because we have to learn lessons."

"Where do we go once we've learned the lessons? What is my lesson?" Sherilyn feels the need to know this.

Place 33, Secrets of Universal Truths Revealed

"Well, right now you're working on judgment. My lesson is humility," Sterling says, "and then we go on to another lesson. We always learn. You decide what you need to learn. We're always with God. It's a never-ending cycle."

"Is there a beginning?" Sherilyn asked.

"Yes. We all began in our minds," he says.

"In the Bible, in Genesis, where it says, 'In the beginning...' What does that mean?" She asks.

"It's about new birth," he replied.

"New birth? Hmm ok, the birth of what? Where it says, 'In the beginning was the word and the word was with God, and the word was God.' What does that mean?" she asked.

Sterling replied, "Thought." "You are all God's thoughts and the highest form of power is energy." We're still floating into a very bright white light; it's like white flowers all melted together creating light. It's a panorama.

"White as far as you can see." Sherilyn repeats.

"So, if you speak words and affirm them, do they come true?"

"If you put feeling into it--put a lot of feeling into the thought you're affirming. It's about having faith." Sterling replies.

"I see. So did you and I come from the same planet? The same beginning?" She asked.

"We're from the same Place," he says. "Place 33 it's a place of righteousness. A good place, a very good place" You had to come, it was your turn!" he exclaimed.

"Huh, What about my children? Are they from the same place?" She asked perplexed.

"No, they're from different places. I don't know if I should let you know that yet." Sterling stutters.

"Can you please tell me, let me know what place they're from? I'm curious" Sherilyn pleads.

"Sally is from the same place as you and I. The other children are from different places because of your misplacement. Margot has a lot to learn. She's from the place she needs to be from. Margot is a good person," Sterling says looking at me.

"I know. I love them with all my heart. Let's stay as long as we can. I never want to leave this place. You never know when we'll be back here again." Then changing subject she says, "That presence is still in my hotel room!"

"Let's go back to the elevator and Level 14 and see about that spirit in your room," Sterling says.

"Okay, Let's go," Sherilyn agrees. So they get out of their bubble spheres and almost instantly, they are at Level 14.

They see the "Place of Wishes" also known as, "City of Movement." The doors are open and there are some picnic tables like they saw before. They go over, sit down and Sterling asks Frank what is going on. "I see Angie now and she's in a good mood." Sterling says.

"She is smiling, elated to be with us." Her gown is wide, as she floats above, taking up more than half the sky. She is slowly descending. "I will ask Frank to come up," Sterling tells Sherilyn.

Sterling stops, and ponders a moment. "I've never asked him to do anything like this," Sterling comments.

Sterling is speaking with Frank, "Is it worth it?" he asks him. He hasn't been here in a while. "Angie sends you her love."

"Sterling, ask Frank about the presence in my hotel room," Sherilyn yells!

"I did," he replied. "It's a thought, part of a thought, trapped in a hotel bathroom. Should we do anything about it Frank? We stumbled upon it back in Las Vegas on 3D Earth."

Frank asks, "Who is it?"

Sterling says, "I don't know, she had a good feel."

Frank looks in, "The Biosphere map," explaining to Sterling. "Her name is Amber. She was only sixteen years old when it happened back in 1820. She had a heart attack and died."

Place 33, Secrets of Universal Truths Revealed

Sherilyn added, "When I looked up at the end of my bed and saw her, she was wearing a weird-looking robe. It was long and blackish red, it looked like something from the 1800's."

Sterling got upset because she's been trapped there almost two centuries. He says, "Good Lord, shit! For Christ sakes, get her out of here Frank. Let her go. Let her go!"

Frank indicates that he will look into it. Angie is just smiling. Frank says, "She's one of the few thoughts left that were trapped."

"Can we help her?" Sherilyn asked again.

Sterling looks at her and says, "Cut the cord. Now!"

"What are you talking about?" she wondered, "Can't you do it Sterling?"

"Pick it up! Pick up the Axe of Light!" He yells out with a sense of urgency.

"Where is the axe?" Sherilyn asks, looking around frantically.

"Pick it up," he says. That's all that's needed. Cut the black cord. Then she'll leave and she can soar."

Confused, Sherilyn asked again, "Where is this Axe of Light?"

"It's lying on the ground," Sterling replied, pointing to the ground.

"Where? I am looking; it is tricky to see in this dimension. There are so few things that are dense in molecular structure," she replied.

Frantically, Sterling shouts, "By the picnic table. It's to the right, actually west, at the end of the picnic table. Its laying right there! Just pick up the axe, cut the cord and she'll leave!"

The grass is white. The picnic table is clear and the axe is clear. The cord that the presence Amber is connected to in the hotel bathroom is black. It is clear inside, but black on the outside.

"Yeah, it's clear, huh? Really easy to see," she says with sarcasm. "Can you do it?" Sherilyn pleaded with him.

Sterling replies supporting her, "You do it, Sherilyn. She's female."

"I guess there's something about female energy. Okay, I got it" Sherilyn says reluctantly. "So, you just swing it? Swing the axe. I am very nervous about this," she says.

Sterling asks her, "Do you see the cord?"

75

"I see something that looks kind of black to white," she answers. She's trying to visualize the cord. It suddenly appears. "Did I hit it?" she asked. Suddenly black dust explodes into the air. The spray from the cord is like graphite dust. Both Sterling and Sherilyn sneeze at the same time from the black-gray dust.

"That was great! The cord was thicker than you thought," Sterling says. "Man, all kinds of shit came off that damn thing! Good God, I wasn't expecting that. There was all kinds of stuff inside that cord."

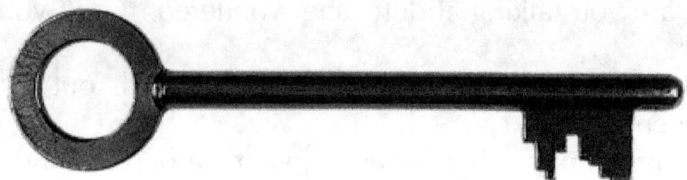

"I thought the cord was supposed to be silver? Amber was here for a long time wasn't she Frank said she was from the 1820's." Sherilyn reiterated.

"Boy she took off fast. Good God!" Sterling says again.

"She didn't even say thank you," Sherilyn says, laughing.

"No way. She's outta here!" Sterling says with a smile.

"I'm glad she's finally gone. At least we could help her," Sherilyn illuminated. "Thank you Frank, thank you Angie, and thank you Sterling."

"As we're walking back to the elevator, Sterling reacts to how fast she shot out of there. "I've never seen that before," he tells her.

"Amazing! Damn that cord was so big. I couldn't believe I actually busted it in two. I swung the axe as hard I could," Sherilyn exclaimed.

"You're more powerful than you think, Sherilyn; you don't always trust your abilities. You believe what you think, but you don't always implement it. You need to open your lens more.

Your lens would fly open just like the presence flew out of that room," he remarked.

"Oh yeah? How?" Sherilyn questions.

Place 33, Secrets of Universal Truths Revealed

"You must believe you can do it. They won't do it for you, because that would interfere with your lesson," Sterling instructs her.

Then Sherilyn says, "Sterling, how about you come over to my place tomorrow? We'll try hypnosis. Let's see if we can get to the Spirit world that way." Sterling agrees, gives her a quick kiss on the cheek, and says goodbye.

When you see the world through your five senses, you are looking at life in the physical world - the world of man. When you see your world symbolically, through the realm of archetypes, you are seeing it from a divine perspective.

Chapter 7 - Look To The Left

Sherilyn is standing outside the door of the elevator. She and Sterling are just getting to know each other. She recalls his instructions to look to the left. The truth is found by looking left. Drinking the truth in is the way to go, she has discovered.

Sterling says, "You must look to the left. Looking left is what people often have the most trouble doing. You do it by letting go. Surrender. That's all you have to do, honestly. People find it difficult to do that. Surrender and be the messenger!"

"Yeah it is hard to do. It's actually scary sometimes," Sherilyn whispers.

Sterling says. "Do you have anything you want to ask me? You can ask for what you need. I'm at peace now."

"Are you at peace, with yourself?" she asks him. "That's what the Christ Consciousness is about, right?"

"Well, it's really more about the Peace Consciousness." Sterling responded.

Changing the subject, Sherilyn tests Sterling, "What should I do about my destiny?"

He replies, "You are all so personal on Earth. You must look to the left, but know how to work the right. It is a balance that must be done that way."

"Can you give it to me in laymen's terms please," she implored.

"What I am saying is actually simple," he says. Just listen to your Intuition. You're wiser than you know. Don't backslide, instead always keep moving forward."

"I don't understand. Should I pray and ask Angie to help me? Pray for wisdom?" Sherilyn probes.

"Angie is smiling on you; she'll help you!" he answers.

"Okay. So I should pray for wisdom?" Sherilyn says with concern.

"The light will correct you. You already know that. You get too personal!" he recapped.

"About my children?" Sherilyn clarifies.

Place 33, Secrets of Universal Truths Revealed

"About your life in general. You're all so personal. You will discover there is an easier way. You will be closer and get closer to God's energy. Just let go, let it be. Get closer to it, and your strength will multiply." Sterling says.

"Do you get closer to it through prayer and meditation?" Sherilyn asks one more time.

"You get closer through understanding how to **look to the left!**" Sterling announces.

"Okay. What does that mean exactly? Look to the left? Surrender?" she asks.

"What you see from the corner of your eyes will be larger than what you see in front," he replies. "It starts out like a glimpse. At first it seems difficult to do. What you're really doing is allowing the light to come through. The more you do it, the larger the light becomes. When you become closer to the truth, your life will become easier. People will be attracted to this truth; then you'll explain it to them."

"Mmm-hmm, I see. Will I be a teacher?" Sherilyn queried.

"You are a teacher. Crystals are from the left. Be sure to open up and build momentum. Keep it up and don't backslide. You worry too much about your children, your life. Let it flow," Sterling instructs.

"Just let it flow, huh?" Sherilyn contemplated his words.

"Yes, what you want is a little complex. Look at Kenton's life; he's always busy. You can learn from him and from others who have a life of complexity. You can gain wisdom without making the same mistake. Don't forget to take a shortcut when you can," Sterling suggests.

He continues, "You're very fortunate. You know that you haven't been hurt more. What happens is if your risk-taking behavior exceeds your ability, regardless of what it is, then you're in extremely dangerous territory. You've done this quite a few times. The marginal reason why you haven't been hurt more is due to Angie's interventions."

"Yes, I know she protects me," Sherilyn answers in reverence.

"You're not far away, don't be so personal. Trust what you know, he emphasizes. "You're getting a bit desperate. Just trust and don't vary from that. You'll be right. Once you understand, it's time to go on to something else. It's like telling time. You don't have to keep relearning."

"Yes, that's true. So what should I learn next?" Sherilyn wonders.

"Trust. That's challenging for you, isn't it?" Sterling reprimands.

"Yes, I have had some really bad relationships. Should I trust Kenton?" she asks.

"Yes," he answers emphatically.

As they talk, they are walking toward the White Sea. There is an extremely large lily pad on the shore. They are naked, about to sit on the lily pad. They feel free in their nakedness and not embarrassed in this dimension.

"Can you see the white water? It's so clean and fresh," Sterling asks.

Sherilyn replies, "Yes. It smells pure; can we drink it?"

"Yes," Sterling says. "Here take this. It's a glass pitcher."

"Where did you get that?" Sherilyn asks surprised.

"It was just there," he says.

"Ah, okay pour me a glass, would you please? Now pour yourself one. Look at the pitcher; you can hardly see the water. It's so pure!" Sherilyn announces.

They both start laughing together. "I love it when you're here. You're very transparent today," Sterling says. "You're willing to give into the truth. The truth is good. Drink the water, drinking the water is so wise."

"My cup runneth over!" Sherilyn cheers.

"Let it soak in, feel it nurture you, Sherilyn. We should drink it more often, every chance we get," Sterling says.

Place 33, Secrets of Universal Truths Revealed

"How do I get here again? The same way we got here on the elevator?" she questions.

"No, that is just a technique. There are many ways," he says. "The important thing is to get there! You have to trust more."

"Trust...more?" she asked perplexed.

"Trust more than yourself. The more you release the need to control the outcome of everything, the more the field which is self-intelligent, self-aware, and self-transcendent can move through you," says Sterling.

She knew he was right though. She could feel resistance in her body. "I've had a lot of bad experiences with trust," she says softly.

"The reason is because you've always had judgment of others in your way. Stop it! And you'll release and be able to trust more easily. It's a new day," he says, smiling. "Let it go. You've finally changed your polarity."

"Okay, I'll try," Sherilyn, says with hesitance.

"Drink the water, drinking the water is connecting you to your higher self," Sterling resonates.

"As we drink the water, our energy changes to a higher frequency." Sherilyn starts hearing that high pitch sound again.

She turns to Sterling and he is exploding with light! He becomes pure consciousness.

"Be pure. Look at the purity by always looking to the left. You haven't been doing it Sherilyn. Let the light come in. Your judgment will improve. Look to the left. Let go and let God. Don't get desperate you might make a mistake. As you see I am, what I am. This is who I truly am. You can refer to me as St. Stephen," says Sterling.

"Wow!!! How beautiful you are. So that's what a consciousness looks like? You have fewer molecules like Angie and you're much larger." Sherilyn clarified.

"Ok, that's my next goal. Let go, release things every day, stop judging others, and trust more," she decided.

Lilly Lounging

By Sherilyn B. Avalon

Place 33, Secrets of Universal Truths Revealed

The Elevator of Light
forgiven people only

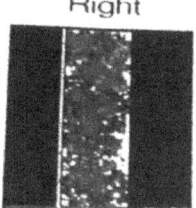

The unforgiven elevator smells and it drips

Elevators Of Forgiven & Unforgiven

Forgiven Mindset.	Unforgiven Mindset
Unconditional Love	Fear, Failure
Positive thoughts	Negative thoughts
Acceptance	Envy
Forgiveness	Controlling Ego
Understanding	Criticism of everything
Compassionate	Negative intent
Objective Vision	Lust
Peace, Purity, Joy	Hate
Do the right thing	Jealousy

In the awareness of our spiritual identity...It is here where we have to see whether we can apply the brakes on patterns of negative thinking, establish and maintain patterns of positive thinking and test whether we have reached the stage where, no person or situation, however negative, can disturb our state of mind.

Chapter 8 - Karmic Tar

Sterling came to visit while the kids were at school. "It feels much better here since the presence left," Sherilyn tells him. "Thank you so much for helping me release it. Are you ready to be hypnotized?" She asked.

Sherilyn starts with, "I have read numerous books on hypnosis and have done some training. I want to see if we can access 'The Place' this way, accessing the 33rd dimension via the spirit world, so to speak." Sterling and Sherilyn get ready to ascend through hypnosis.

Before being taken into the spirit world, Sterling asks, "Do you have a beer, or perhaps a glass of wine?"

"Sure," she says. "It's probably good to loosen up a bit." The list of questions she wants to ask him suddenly blurs. Obviously, Sterling is having an effect on her. Sherilyn feels like an amateur, sitting next to this man who is like a god, since she found out who he really is. Once she gets her bearings, She pulls herself together, even though the other man she really wanted to be with cancelled their date.

Part of her wanted Kenton and part of her wants to make love with Sterling. After several minutes of small talk, she asks Sterling to tell her what the symbols of his tattoos mean. She was simply curious, not prying.

Standing up, Sterling removed his shirt, handed it to her, and then sat down, closer to her. She could not help but notice Sterling's bare skin and how smooth it looked. His stomach and chest muscles were tight. His blonde hair hung loose, blowing in the breeze from the fan. He points to a large round tattoo. He says, "This is the flower of life. It represents the creation pattern, the way in, the way out. This one is a crown, to remember I'm in charge of my royalty and I can't forget Mom."

"Wow!" Sherilyn knew she could not allow her sexual thoughts to linger for another second. Immediately she changed her focus. She crisply instructs Sterling, "Let's get started." She gently lulls Sterling into a conscious hypnotic state. While in a trance, it's crucial to make sure the vibrations

Place 33, Secrets of Universal Truths Revealed

which are in the higher dimensions, are planned in an exact sequence, or he could get lost in his mind. This is especially true in the thirty-third dimension. She realizes she can talk to Sterling and others while actually in this dimension, in the spirit world.

"Get ready for another great adventure," he says. They are in the elevator. Sherilyn starts counting down to Level 33. They are at The Place, so they go to the lily pads and fill themselves with the white water. They are pure again for now.

Sterling says, "Early on, when we went to the other side of The Place, I told you about the Unforgiven, remember?"

"Mmm hmm," she replies.

"You take a damp, stinky, rotting elevator to get there," he says. "Oh that side is where the unforgiven souls hang out. They must become saturated with negativity before going to the forgiven side."

"Right, let's go check it out," Sherilyn says. They are back in the elevator.

He says, "Push number eight."

They are on Level Eight instantly. Now they're transporting themselves to the opposite side of eight. They are getting out on the left side of the elevator. The other side of the elevator door opens this time.

"We're going to enter into the left hemisphere. First we must get to the center of my mind," Sterling says.

"Okay, how do we do that?" Sherilyn asks confused.

"The Pathway is right there. All you do is open the door," Sterling informs me. "We look out the window and see the pool." I am visualizing this entire experience with him.

"The door is open," Sherilyn says.

"This is it. Give me a piece of paper, please," Sterling asks.

"It seems so far away, like drawing with a 30-foot pencil. How large is this paper? Please be calm so I can center myself." Sterling directs Sherilyn.

"Okay," She says handing him piece of paper and a pencil. His eyes are firmly closed.

Sterling proceeded to draw a map on the paper. "The elevator is here, 33 floors are over here, and then turn there.

We'll get off here. This would've gone down to the eighth floor. Okay, always remember, take me back exactly the way we came or I'll be confused. I want you to get into the new elevator of shadow with me. This is the Unforgiven elevator; the elevator's in the left hemisphere in the center of my mind!"

"Okay I'm getting in with you. Where are we going?" She asks, visualizing all of it.

"We are going down to Level 33," Sterling states. "All right, we're here. Open the door. God, it's beautiful!" He says.

Startled, Sherilyn asks him, "What does it look like?"
Since he's in a conscious hypnotic trance and she's here in 3D Earth, she can't see it exactly as he sees it. But, she can visualize it. She uses her imagination, which she found out is real.

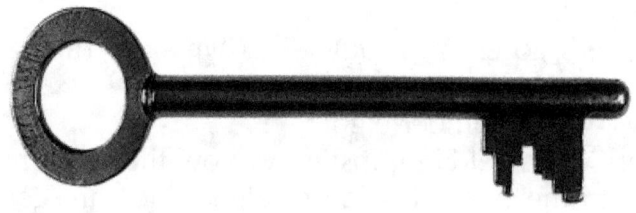

"Beautiful, gorgeous. It's an iridescent blue-black sea. It's stunning. Absolutely a deep, indigo blue-black iridescent onyx color," says Sterling. "The depth of color reflects the depths which we're at. It's the opposite of light. Logically in a conscious mind you would think it's in the left, representing white and light. But the nature of the mirror principle flips it into reverse. Its Frank's doing of course."

"Interesting," he says looking through the window. "Let's sit down over there," he says pointing left.

"Is there a lily pad there?" Sherilyn asks. It's strange, even though she's not actually there; She senses she's there. "One of my other bodies are there, I feel the energy there," she says, "I can visualize, what's happening. It's extraordinary," she acknowledges.

Place 33, Secrets of Universal Truths Revealed

"Open the door, please," Sterling says. "It's certainly different, that's for sure."

Welcome to "Karmic Tar," Sterling bellows. "I'm ready to be here now. I had to be filled with light to such a degree so I can explore here without danger. There's a lot of dark clouds overhead. They aren't menacing; they have a shimmering quality. Everything has a translucent look. It's quite beautiful. If I wasn't from the light it would be menacing, but it's not. I can be fairly objective about it. You must always remember the riddle of the left and right. It's always in reverse."

"Okay, I'll remember that," Sherilyn remarked.

"It's that way because we're meant to know the truth." But, we have to progress far enough to figure it out. Those who should know it are the ones to know it. That way they can't do any damage by using the knowledge incorrectly.

You asked about the lily pads. No lily pads here--there are black boxes instead," Sterling comments.

"Black boxes? What are they made of?" asks Sherilyn.

"Black mahogany. But at the bottom of the box there's black lava-like glass. The mahogany sides are sitting on the glass, penetrating it. I'm telling you what I see. I think it would burn people who aren't from the light," Sterling describes to Sherilyn.

"Is that right? Are we sitting on it? On the box?" she asked.

"Yes, but instead of putting our feet in the water, we're reaching our feet skyward. We're sitting down in it, with our feet up as far as we can point them," he says.

"Isn't that uncomfortable?" Sherilyn quinces.

"Yes, it's somewhat uncomfortable. But, this way we can soak up all the energy," Sterling exclaims.

Excitedly, she asks, "Really, soak up the energy of what?" Little did she know what she was diving into?

"The mystery of the Kingdom of God," Sterling answers. "Now we have to soak up the darkness."

"What's in the darkness?" Sherilyn asks perplexed.

Sterling replies, "There's a great deal of knowledge in the darkness. It's uncomfortable but it's necessary for balance.

Your hands are black, you have black fingernail polish, your lips are black, your tongue is black, and your hair is black and sticky. Oh, and you have bad breath."

"What about you, same thing? Is my body black?" Sherilyn questioned.

"Yes, our bodies are bluish-black. Our souls have absorbed the energy of this place." Sterling pauses and adds, "You want to know how to purify your soul, right?"

"Yes, I do," Sherilyn radiates.

"Remain true to what you know and you'll purify yourself. Just don't think you can do what you want when you want to, just because you can Sherilyn. It's a matter of self-discipline. This will help you purify your soul. You'll purify your body with the organic chemical agents you use. You'll also purify with herbs from Chinese medicine to help with un-pure thoughts resulting from guilty reactions. You've met your Karmic catalyst," Sterling resonates.

"Are we filled with this stuff yet?" Sherilyn queries.

"No, it's thick. We're about one-third full. We're being filled with gooey, black tar-like stuff," Sterling states.

"Yuck, do we have to do this?" She thinks while visualizing this.

"Yeah, it's a refresher," he says.

"A refresher? How could any of this be refreshing?" she asks.

"Don't let my words fool you," he says. "Think about the opposite of refresh, what is it?"

"To be laden?" she answers, quickly looking it up on her cell phone.

"Yes, please understand the value of the riddle," he says.

"I know. There are riddles in the Bible, too." Sherilyn interjects.

Sterling says, "Actually when I'm on this side of the veil you can call me St. Stephan. When I'm in 3D Earth, I'm Sterling."

Sterling's higher self, St. Stephan, is speaking now through Sterling.

Place 33, Secrets of Universal Truths Revealed

"Okay, so when 'St. Stephan' speaks, that means he is speaking from The Place, and when you say, 'Sterling is speaking', he is speaking from above in 3D Earth, in reality. As above, so below right?" Sherilyn inquired.

"Yes, Sterling loves you in a pure, almost cosmic way. On some days he configures energy so you are protected. He speaks with Angie for you." St. Stephan relays.

"Do I need it?" She cajoles.

"Yes," St. Stephan says, "Due to your earlier spiritual misplacement you lack the essential skills you could have tapped into at this stage. This is what happened to you. It's particularly true since you met Sterling. He was pivotal for you. He literally changed the course of your life from negative to positive. It's by no means over."

"That's pretty amazing." Sherilyn murmured.

"This is dense, thick 'Karmic Tar,'" St. Stephan says.

"We're halfway full now. We're sinking and sinking. We've gone through the glass bottom. It's like someone has thrown us in with lead tied to our feet."

Sherilyn starts coughing and says, "What a shocking revelation. I feel like I'm about to drown. Are we going under?" She asks, still coughing.

"Yes, it's certainly a smothering experience. But it's a refresher for the Truth; it's a good thing." Sterling laughs as he comments.

"Are we coming here again?" She asks, sputtering the words as she coughs.

"Sterling loves you to death," St. Stephan speaks again. "You're connected by a cord of light that's quite secure. You're my daughter. Random fate could always alter it, of course. Odds are against it by far."

"Sterling is my Spiritual Father?" Sherilyn asks, taken aback.

"Yes, in a sense. The consciousness that I am is your father through me, we operate within the same spirit family," St. Stephan replies.

"Ok, We are sitting here with nothing to do, but fill up with this Karmic Tar stuff. So I want to ask you some questions. Can you tell me about the Convergence?" she inquires.

"The convergence of the conscious and the unconscious mind that is at hand-- the timing is correct. There is a percentage of souls that will dictate it. There will be an Osmosis that occurs and it'll coincide with much happening all over the world with many people now. It's an inevitable fusion of unification. It's a natural evolution for all, with you as the catalyst. What you've involved Sterling in relative to the hypnosis sessions is important too. These sessions allow the hallmark of metaphysics intention. Sterling's always been kind of a canary in the mine for these things. So are you!" St. Stephan explains.

"I am?" Sherilyn asks, taken aback again.

"Just not quite as much. You would've been just as much of a canary as Sterling if this error hadn't occurred. First, you must expand your consciousness into the higher dimensions," says St. Stephan.

Sherilyn starts coughing again and asks, "What about Odin? I dreamt about him the other night."

"St. Stephan was familiar with Odin in other lifetimes because he's part of him. Odin was a force for truth, purity and cosmic awareness —a strikingly powerful force and a force of leadership. Odin's power ties in with fire, the planet Mars, and inertia," replies St. Stephan.

"How about making a Talisman? I was contemplating making one. What do you think of that idea?" Sherilyn questions him.

"A butterfly talisman for you would be good...powerful and magnifying," St. Stephan conveys through Sterling.

"I love butterflies! How far are we in the box? I'm so-o-o ready to go," Sherilyn says, hoping she won't have to do this when she returns after transcending.

"We're almost there. We've almost sunk to the bottom. It's making me sleepy because I'm so weighted down," Sterling says speaking from atop.

Place 33, Secrets of Universal Truths Revealed

"I'll wake you up!" Sherilyn cries, "in fear we might be stuck there forever." It seemed so real.

"I can't breathe!" Sherilyn gasped, coughing uncontrollably.

"We do not need to breathe here; you feel smothered. We have black bodies, with tar-like sticky eyes and hair even though we are not wearing clothing. We feel burdened more than wet. It is thick, heavy goo. Movement forward is difficult. We are almost saturated now. Once thoroughly drenched we will start moving back up toward the surface. Then we can climb back through the mahogany boxes and finally out. Not something done very often," St. Stephan relays.

"I want to get out of here, let's go," Sherilyn screams, as they make grunting noises, moving through the gooey, throbbing, black liver-like stew. Now that liver is mentioned. Sherilyn asks, "What do you do to clean your liver? Your physical liver."

"St. Stephan replies, "Reduce stress and drink a lot of distilled water. Ginseng helps, as well as vitamin C. Avoid fat and alcohol in the diet. Take hydrogen and niacin. Take a sauna when you can. You will feel much healthier; you won't believe the difference."

"Uh, are we filled with the gunk yet?" Sherilyn keeps asking.

"Oh yeah, we are definitely filled. We are one with the gunk. It's like tar; it's carbon-based like people are carbon based. But more than people, it is extremely dense and highly weighted. It's a dark type of carbon molecule that makes up the sea. It tastes like sour, ashen, gagging, living dust. It's a very dark carbon molecule. It is a retching, wet, thick dust, a horrible thing. We can do it because we're equipped to avoid suffocation.

We are on top now! We are okay, we are there, and we are finally on top of the mahogany box." Sterling reveals through his hypnotic state.

"That was depressing. I'm so glad we're out," Sherilyn exclaims.

"You actually have tar coming out of your nose," Sterling says laughing at me with his eyes closed.

"Here let me wipe some on you. I don't like this stuff," Sherilyn says, giggling. She wipes her nose and playfully pretends to smear some of the black ooze on him. He's already covered in it anyway, she figured, laughing at him. "It's the concrete." Sterling mentions quietly. "We had to get saturated with it. We're still covered in tar; let's slowly go back. I don't need to be here anymore. Get back in the elevator and let's go to Level eight. Take me back the way we came, please. Then let's check out level four," Sterling says with a smile.

In his unconscious hypnotized state, Sterling is visualizing both of us all yucky and covered in black goo. But Sherilyn felt it. She must be living it out on another dimension, she thought to herself, feeling it on this 3rd dimension. It was so weird.

St. Stephan says, "I will introduce the 33 dimensions now. One through eight are mathematical, based on physics and science. The rest are more complex. Now we are ready to transport to other Levels. We have traveled in the elevator and we are going past all the Levels." The elevator slows down by each level, one by one.

Level one is the first. It's a tunnel of energy. You enter it and you can conform to the walls. Other souls are in there. The energy goes through you. The other levels are hard to explain. They are like a hue within a hue, an abstract, abstract maze.

Level Two is cherry flavored. Children souls go here after their mother had an abortion, or if they die too soon. It's rainbow-colored and a very shallow place.

Now we are passing Level Three, where we are from, the 3rd dimension.

Sterling says, "I see your stepfather, Robert on Level Four. He is waiting to come back, but not yet. He appears content and happy with himself."

Sherilyn asked, "Is he still smoking cigars? My mom and brother smelled cigars in the house not long after he made his transition. He must have visited them one day."

Place 33, Secrets of Universal Truths Revealed

"Yeah, he wants to come back," Sterling answers. "This is uncomfortable, because he wants to pass through me. I'm uneasy with it. His emotions are tied to his last life. With respect to his life in general, he needs to move on. He needs to let go completely."

"The elevator is at Level Four," Sterling says, "I'm looking out the window and see an awesome labyrinth-type maze."

"It's the Green Labyrinth of Wisdom," Sterling replies.

Sterling says, "we've traveled to a red maze. It's part of a large spiritual estate."

"Where is it located?" Sherilyn probes.

Sterling acknowledges, "It is directly south from the center of where we are." The elevator stops. They get out and explore. Sterling begins wandering through the circular maze. "It is warm in here," he says. The outer trim of the walls is burning red and the walls are lime green. There is a trap door under the floor. "At the end, I see water under it."

"Let's jump in the water and get cleaned off. Get all this Karmic Tar off us," Sherilyn suggests, and then asks, "What is the maze for?"

"It's a mansion. There's a maze in the front yard for testing your wits, testing your sense of direction," Sterling replies.

"Cool! When Biblical scholars say, 'There are mansions built in heaven' is this one of them?" Sherilyn retorts.

"I find walking the Labyrinth easy, as if I've done it many times before. I'm having fun going through it over and over again. I enjoy looking at its design. It kind of looks like it could be from France, originating in the Middle Ages." Sterling interposes.

"The purpose of the labyrinth is to determine if you can get through it okay. It's nice, cool, and green. It's refreshing."

"Does everyone have to go through it when they transcend?" Sherilyn asked with trepidation.

"No, not everyone. Only those souls wise enough to be tested," he responded.

"Have I been through it?" she asked.

"Yes, your name's on a plaque for having successfully completed it. The plaque is inlaid into the oak trunk of a tree.

There are hundreds of trees all around with inlaid plaques," Sterling says.

"How many plaques are there?" She queried.

"There are 444 plaques," he replied.

"Okay does my plaque say my name? What does it say on my plaque?" she asks.

"It says Cherlyn. Then in parentheses it says (Sherilyn Bridget). It indicates the effect you can have on your fate through your own will. In your case, you took the opportunity to affect the outcome of your fate through your will. You have two names," Sterling illustrated.

"Which name shall I use?" she probes.

"It's like looking at the lines on your palm, mapping your life and others. Your fate was to be with a 'C' but the effect is with an 'SB' that's why it's in parentheses."

"What about my last name, Avalon?" she asks.

"The name Avalon represents the apple, choice energy," he replied.

"Choice energy? If I stopped using the name Avalon would I have less choice energy?" she inquired. They are now walking at the raw red outer edge of the Labyrinth.

"There is a blank on the question of your last name. It appears to be left open. It reflects things yet to come," Sterling says.

"The letter 'S' suggests an understanding of infinity. It connects up creating the number eight. If you reverse Sterling's 'S' in his name and the 'S' in your name, you have two halves of infinity working together…" declares St. Stephan.

"I like that." Sherilyn smiled.

"Both of you are teachers and leaders. Sterling is the more experienced one at this point," St. Stephan remarked.

"Sterling wants to know why he is experiencing so much pain in his physical body. He wanted me to ask his God-self since he doesn't quite know how to access you yet." I muse to St. Stephan.

Sterling's higher self, St. Stephan, communicates via Sterling that it's a karmic debt. "The physical pain is part of his sacrificial debt. He is paring down his debts with sacrifice. His

Place 33, Secrets of Universal Truths Revealed

Karmic debt is also tied into past lives as well as the one he is currently living. Gradually he is chipping away at his fundamental lesson, which is complete humility, a difficult lesson. This should be his last time through the cycle.

Sterling is too smart to achieve humility simply through his interaction with people, because he is always outsmarting them. So his health was imposed upon to learn the lesson at a deeper level.

He is suffering to a degree that he can handle it, and still remain attentive to completing the lesson fully. He will experience challenge with it for the rest of his life.

There is Sterling's <u>emotional reaction</u> to the injuries; his <u>attitude</u> is vital and <u>intent</u> which creates the three parts or the triad to the lesson."

"Is there always a triad to each lesson?" Sherilyn asks St. Stephan, through Sterling as they continue descending into the levels in their minds.

"Yes, Sterling's known for most of his life that any part of the puzzle or strategy doesn't work alone. It works in conjunction with the other integral parts, just like a game of chess. Three is one of the most powerful numbers because it creates a vortex. In that vortex, energy is funneled and focused. Turn it upside down until it is full, then when you are ready to project what is inside of it, it is turned right side up again," St. Stephan continues.

"So the triangle is like a pyramid?" Sherilyn queried.

"No 'the triad' is geometric," St. Stephan replies. "Yet the geometric form holds information. The container is concrete and solid. There is information contained within the triad creating a duality, its abstract knowledge held within. The wisdom inside can be shot out anytime towards anything. Always use the vortex triad. Just like the pyramid, the triangle acts as a concrete structure. It funnels down and attracts the information you are attempting to attract. Then it is turned right side up.

That way information is funneled and focused out of the apex of the linear triad form."

"I have another question. Why is Angie cloaked with miraculous robes and Frank is naked?" Sherilyn asks inquisitively. I'm tired of walking around in the maze, 'the green labyrinth of wisdom with the raw red edge'. I want to sit on the edge of the wall." Sherilyn noticed that the most favored nymphs are flying around, lighting about her simply because she mentioned Angie's name. Sherilyn noticed she sends out little extensions of herself like feelers."

St. Stephan asks her, "Do you see the staircase?"

"No, I don't see it," she answers, and then asks, "Is there really a stairway to heaven though?"

St. Stephan answers, "There are 33 steps on this staircase, but they don't exactly climb to heaven. The stairway leads to a particular place in the Northwest. There are 33 levels of consciousness as you know."

Angie is with us now." Sherilyn looks up saying, "Hi Angie, I love you. Do you like the painting I created of you?"

"She likes how you incorporated her in a real sense within the realm you're living," St. Stephan says. "She also says as you continue with your artwork things will culminate and her influence will be magnified." She says, "the more you work, the more influential your work will become."

"Shall I work with watercolors or oils?" Sherilyn contemplated.

"She likes watercolors for now. Eventually you'll have room for expansion relative to your interest in different artistic mediums," he says.

"Your spiritual father will know when these junctures arise. He will be sure to indicate when it's time to incorporate more," Angie relays telepathically.

"Frank is pleased because he didn't think you saw him as benevolent. He's pleased and he's laughing. He believes your fear is preventing you from actively portraying who he is and how he looks," St. Stephan adds.

"But, does he like it?" she asks.

St. Stephan continues, "Of course, because you're not exposing him for who he authentically is.... *a slick, shiny, deep, infinitely layered, complicated, implementer of ultimate*

Place 33, Secrets of Universal Truths Revealed

un-wisdom. Frank's teaching them, inundating them, and finally, saturating them with the truth."

"To make people stumble and fall?" Sherilyn replies, upset.

"Yeah! That's his job, according to how he sees it should be done," he replies. "He makes people repeat lessons over and over again because he's a perfectionist. Finally they're so saturated there's no room left for thinking or believing differently. Then they can move up the next rung on the ladder in consciousness."

"Well, is he like what people think the devil is? It sounds like how he teaches. That's okay isn't it?" Sherilyn asked.

"It's not necessary," St. Stephan replies. "It's certainly not an absolute. At least that's what Angie and I feel. If you can, just consciously perceive the higher dimensions."

"Can Angie please answer my question? Why does she wear clothing, her robes?" Sherilyn probes.

"She says this is an effortless answer. She wears clothing because Frank wants to see her naked," Stephan replies.

Sherilyn bursts into peals of laughter. "He wants to see an Archetypal Consciousness naked?"

"Uh huh. Frank was about to laugh too, but when she answered he quickly became still." St. Stephan says.

"What would happen if Frank saw her naked?" Sherilyn quizzed, trying unsuccessfully to suppress her giggles.

"Angie believes Frank should adhere to his own ways and his influence on people. So, she won't disrobe in front of him. She's using his approach on him. She believes in allowing him to become saturated with his unnecessary, redundant, repetitive teaching methodology. He would benefit greatly from seeing Angie nude. But, she won't permit it because she feels then he wouldn't learn his own lesson," St. Stephan reveals. "So Frank can imagine what he wants, since he enjoys making things difficult on people. Angie is cloaked in The Truth. Yet it's not the clothing that matters; it's what's beneath. She will show you herself if you ask her. She will allow you to gaze if you want."

"Okay, remember when you told me Angie was 42. Why is Angie 42?" Sherilyn asked.

"She's 42 because every 42 cycles she comes closer to the edge of the parameter, the parameter I won't say we're all trapped in, but presently we're limited by it.

Once we've entered, let's say we've gone beyond the new change. Then, the 3D Matrix of your body expands to integrate these perceptions. Then she'll open her sphere. It appears to be the 13th sphere, which is unknown now. There will be a metamorphosis, a whole new set of circumstances going forward. She has an affinity for 42," St. Stephan answers patiently.

"She is so beautiful at 42 years old," Sherilyn remarks.

"The most beautiful 42 year old you'll ever set eyes upon. Of course, she has an affinity for sixes and nines too," St. Stephan, added.

"What about eights?" Sherilyn quizzes.

"Eight is about universal truth incorporating two halves. Angie's half of a whole herself. Eight is represented in a personification not yet completely formed. It may never be formed because of the limitations we're all living and working with regarding perfection and imperfection.

The birth of eight, well, it's a type of permanence you don't want. Even the thought of it isn't appealing. Things are to be open-ended. For example nine represents a precipice, even though it also represents wisdom," replies St. Stephan.

"Why does nine represent wisdom?" Sherilyn asks.

"Nine is linked to threes, in multiples.

These are representative of knowledge; but ten equates with completion. It has a connection with strategizing things. Nothing is ever complete for very long. So the number ten has

Place 33, Secrets of Universal Truths Revealed

its own self-limiting qualities as a number that represents its completion.

Nine speaks more to the truth than ten, especially regarding the usual manner everything is and always will be," relayed St. Stephan. "Wow! In school we put the numbers zero through nine on a piece of paper, in a straight line vertically, and then put nine through zero in a column vertically beside it. Regardless, they will always add up to nine." Sherilyn gave her little input.

"Oh, incidentally Angie wants you to know there was a 'Linear Awakening.' She's holding up a plaque. It looks like ivory script. She says it occurred May 5th in the year 2000," St. Stephan informed us.

"Is the plaque round or square?" Sherilyn asks.

Sterling replies, "Angie says, the information is round, but the plaque is rectangular.

Frank likes teaching in limited parameters, and then he reveals abstract truths through clearly in-the-box methods of understanding. He likes building various boxes of information. Frank sees no reason to stop, because it's been working for so long.

Angie doesn't disagree with Frank because, it's incorrect to disagree with a format that's been working so long. She simply feels it's unnecessary. Feel is the appropriate term because she's a feeling entity, as opposed to an instructive, moralizing entity like Frank," St. Stephan described.

"When did Frank start? Was it from the beginning of time? That kind of reminds me of the Bible story of Cane and Abel? Was Frank, Cane?" Sherilyn quizzed St. Stephan.

"Well yeah, Frank is the Patriarch of Energy and is to remain just that," St. Stephan answers. "However, that role is now in jeopardy of changing. Think within the context of what appears on the surface in direct opposition to the light. Then you'll have a basic understanding of how Frank teaches with saturation, negativity, and pain--not so things remain negative and perpetually self-destruct, but so they grow saturated and change to the positive, which is why he's a forgiven entity. This is how humans tend to learn." Frank believes.

"So if Frank is Cane, then are you Abel?" Sherilyn questioned St. Stephan.

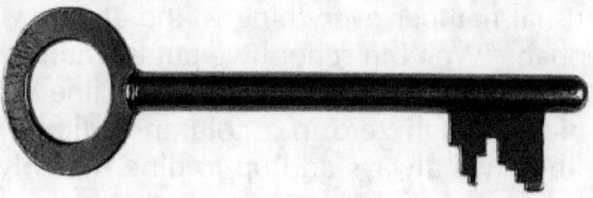

"Yes, I'm the flip side of that same half--like there's a good twin and an evil twin, if you look at it objectively," St. Stephan sighs.

"Does Angie have a flip side?" Sherilyn questions him again.

"Yes, of course. Her name is Sabrina, a black witch. You don't know her. She rules the underbelly of the Light. There are always two halves to a whole, even if the whole is divided in half. Bluntly, if you keep analyzing and splitting halves you discover there are infinite halves, extended into a new, uncharted dimension. This is why Angie likes the number 42. I'm teaching you with threes and nines," St. Stephan adds.

"I thought I was infinitely eight spiritually," she queries St. Stephan.

"You are, but if we allow it to remain, progress would end, continuing to duplicate itself. It would result in an eternal repetition. Incidentally, I'm tapped into the same pool of information with the same amount of clarity as Joseph Campbell, the author of many books. Author Emmett Fox was tapped into more of the feeling pool as contrasting to the data pool.

"I always liked Emmett Fox's works. We just passed Level 12!" Sherilyn exclaimed.

"Hmm,

Place 33, Secrets of Universal Truths Revealed

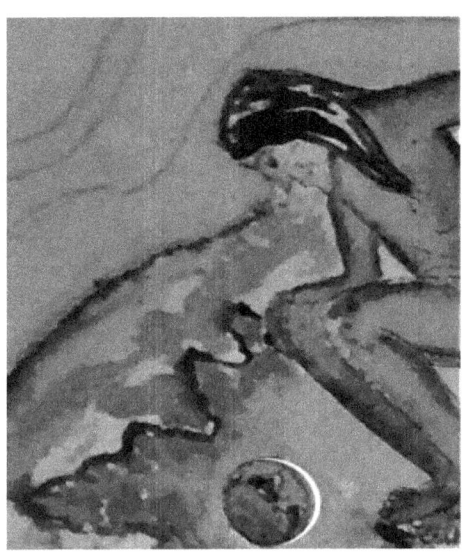

Level 12 was green. Everything is green inside. We are still traveling down the shaft of the elevator, slowly, peaking through the window. There is level 18; it's black and it's empty, and has a hollow sort of feel to it. That's weird; I just see eyes. It looks like souls that are waiting."

"You must learn to integrate your expanded 3D Matrix into Gaia's 3D Matrix. Then, Gaia's 3D Matrix will expand. I will leave you with that." St. Stephan announces as the Elevator stops.

Once again Sherilyn has discovered so much, this time accessing the pool, the levels of the Elevator, through hypnotizing Sterling in her living room. She thanks him for his willingness to go there. He smiles, kisses her tenderly on the lips and leaves

Place 33, Secrets of Universal Truths Revealed

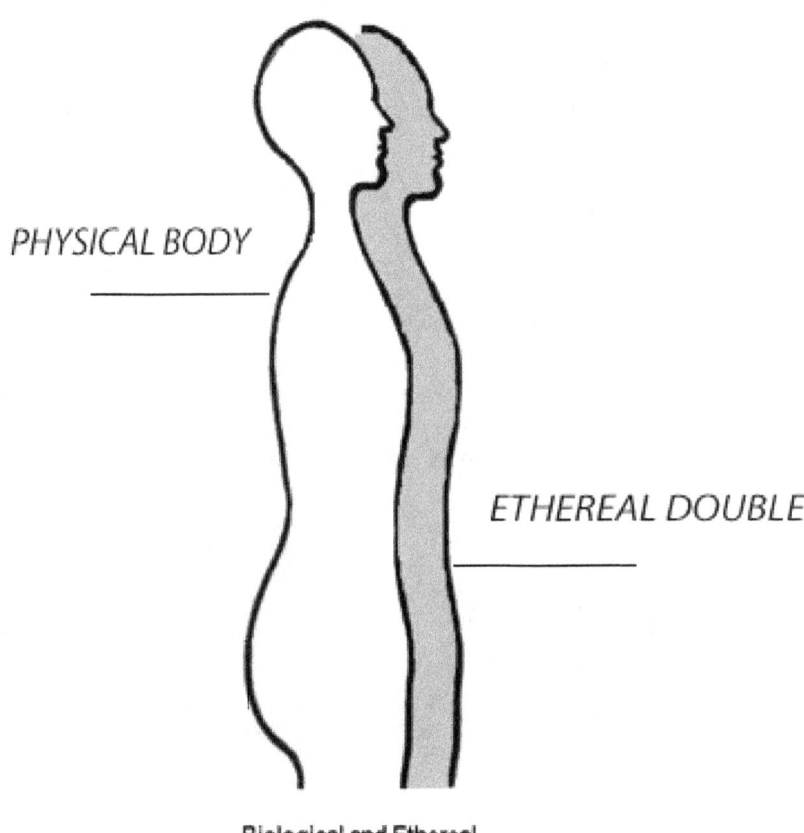

Biological and Ethereal

Sherilyn Bridget Avalon

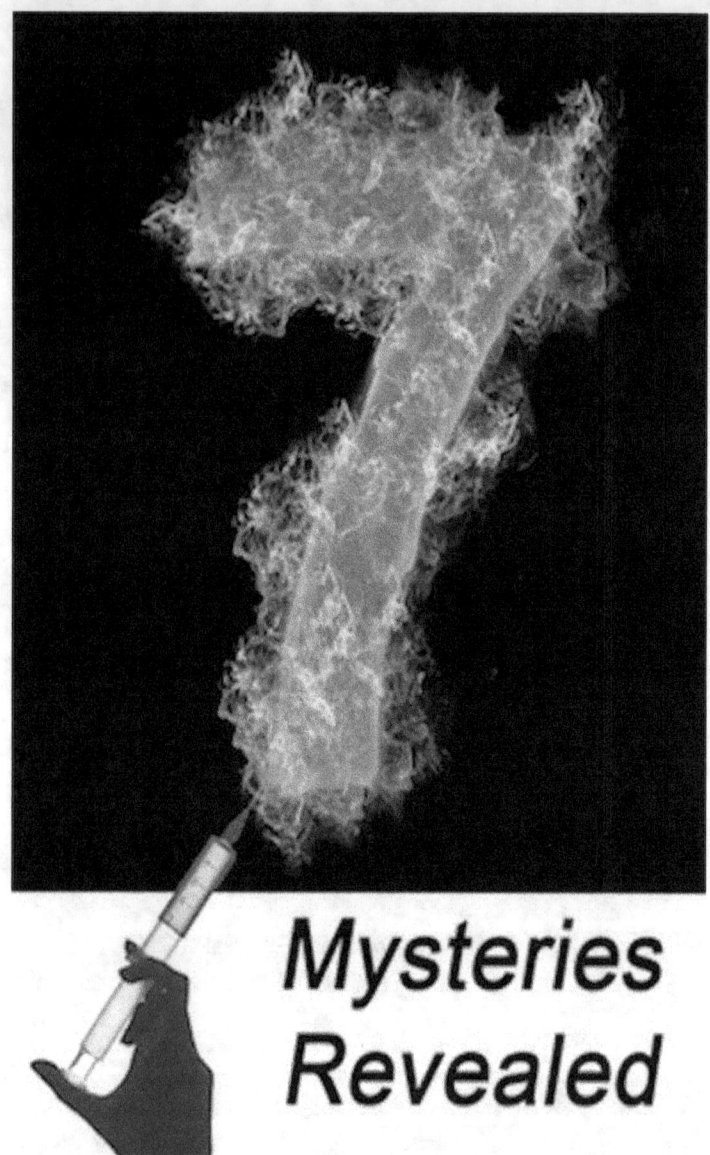

Mysteries Revealed

Place 33, Secrets of Universal Truths Revealed

Chapter 9 – Mysteries Revealed

Sherilyn looks out the window and sees today is a beautiful day.

She and her friend Charity drive south to Sedona, Arizona. They met with a Medium. When he was a little boy he was struck by lightning and then became psychic. His name is Jananda and he is well known among psychics in Sedona.

Jananda tells Charity and Sherilyn, "The Angels say surrender. Just say 'God, I'm ready!' Meditation every day will help. Visualize and connect with the six-point star. Use Tarot cards. Make choices and people will show up; miracles will show up. Have you been thinking about becoming a healer? You can create miracles. Your life and your potential is like Opportunity Junction. Don't be afraid of going with Source. You're currently in a process of transformation, like a butterfly releasing itself from its cocoon."

Sherilyn asks Jananda about her parents, family, and about forgiveness.

"Visualize your Mom and Dad in meditation," he replied. "Look them in the eyes, thank them and set them free. I see the Angel of miracles. You're supposed to be a messenger. You're here to do this work. You're surrounded with beings of light, and, *beings of less light have been assigned to throw you off track.* Surrender to positive, benevolent feelings. "We are here," she says. "Do good things for your kids. Ask your angels to help your children. The 'angelic swat team' can and will assist your daughter. Ask them to help for her highest good. Maybe they'll hit her with a cosmic two by four. She's rebellious."

"Your Granddad is here. Did he wear a cap like a French painter? Did you buy shoes with him? Was it difficult getting the right size? He was helping you select shoes.

He was a cobbler's assistant, his Father was the Cobbler, and he has excellent taste in shoes." (She did find an adorable pair of shoes the day before.)

"Your Granddad is following the family, trying to help your daughter.

Tell her how important it is to eat well...Vitamins B6, B12, folic acid, and liquid trace minerals. There are fat molecules in her blood, maybe cholesterol. It'll help her recover."

"Thank you, Jananda. You gave me confirmation." Sherilyn exclaimed.

They head back to Las Vegas. When they arrive back home Sterling is sitting in the hotel lobby waiting for Sherilyn. "I need to be hypnotized again, the Elevator of Light is broken. I have questions I need answered," Sterling demands.

"Okay, Margot and Sally are at my Mom's house," she replies. "Let me call her and tell her I'll pick them up tomorrow. Mom told me, Granddad was a cobbler's son. I already knew he was an artist. Wow! That was freaky."

In her living room, Sterling knocks on the door. She reminds him she has plans to see Kenton tonight. He seems a little jealous. She told Sterling not to worry. One day he will understand who you are.

"Okay let's get ready for hypnosis. Lie comfortably on the couch, take your shoes off, and relax. I'm counting down from one to 33. One, two, three..." she counts methodically.

"I've crossed over," he says. "I feel good looking at the white water in The Place. I left the friction behind; I feel okay now. It feels better here on Earth. You've got a lot of friction around you, Sherilyn."

"Okay, what are you doing now?" she asks him.

Sterling replies, "I'm just looking at the water. It's so white, and I like looking at it. I can see from whence I came. I also can see my best sphere coming. I see it coming. My mind's been full of spheres today--the sphere of integration, the sphere lacking time and space. When that sphere enters me I'll be different. It's settled on me. It's been a meditative day."

"I missed you Sherilyn, I like your mind. You understand in a fundamental way what's going on. You're interested in the mystery of being, even though you don't articulate in the same language."

Sterling says, "There is a gold tape circling and orbiting me."

"A gold tape. What's that for?" she asked.

Place 33, Secrets of Universal Truths Revealed

"The tape has information on it," Sterling answered.

Then St. Stephan steps in and speaks, "It says Mary is blue and Christ is red. On Earth, Sterling's been thinking about color. I'm giving him permission to peer into the mythological yet truthful anecdotes throughout history.

Imagination speaks to our psyche. So, in terms of insight it's valid. Major religions understand this, if it's well understood. That's why Mythology is linked to imagination like a pathway made by an animal. It's like following animal tracks. They are tracks to the truth. These tracks speak to the mystery of being.

With human tracks they link to the human psyche. That's why the groundbreaking, Dr. Carl Jung, tried putting things in psychological terms for Western man to understand. It was difficult, yet, understandable.

Even the 'Tibetan Book of the Dead' revealed the truth to a point. Eventually time and space took over. So if there can be no thought, there can be no thought about it.

The practice of Christianity is often in conflict with, and opposite to integration. This has been true for too many years. It will change soon. There's a vital, connected relationship between man, nature and spirit. This speaks to a lack of understanding about how the universe is truly structured, a major flaw.

I see Kundalini yoga on the tape. There's coiled information in the form of two snakes. Two snakes are climbing a pole. They are female snakes starting at the base under the tailbone. They're crawling up the spine to the top of the head. At the crown of the head, I see many gold things."

"What do they represent?" she asks St. Stephan.

"It represents an absence of ego, St. Stephan replied.

"It's about the second being next to all of us. It's about time and space. Remove time and space we're all connected. Once in a while there's a true metaphysical phenomenon. It's the reason why a man who doesn't know a child trapped in a house fire, will completely forget his ego, himself, his natural instinct for survival, and blindly save a child or an adult. It's not because he wants a reward or recognition. For a split second he breaks through, and reconnects with his oneness. He believes, he's saving himself and doesn't know the difference.

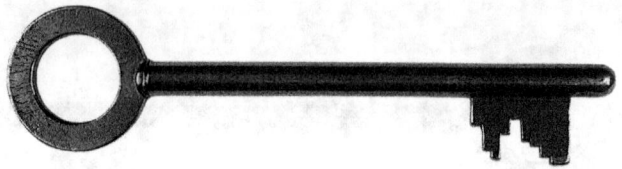

Information is passing by on the gold tape. The tape references Lunar and Solar consciousness. The moon and sun are metaphors for different types of light and energy. Man's perception of God through the world's religions is simply a personification of energy, attaching human traits to diverse types of energy. God is energy. Our shallow attempt to define God through religion will never rise above time and space."

"Is there any way to rise above time and space?" Sherilyn asked.

"Yes, it's by understanding direction," St. Stephan answers. "Time and space are the two most important concepts to understand if we're going to truly understand 'The Mystery of Being.'"

"Do you mean North, South, East and West?" she asks.

"Correct," he replies. "Also you'll always come closer to understanding through numbers rather than through words. Direction and numbers are better mediums of communication and understanding."

"I have a friend, Mike Kurban who does numerology. He's always right on with numbers," she interjects.

Place 33, Secrets of Universal Truths Revealed

"The gold tape is like reading a tablet," he continues. "Wait, the tape has stopped. It's both lunar consciousness and solar consciousness. The lunar consciousness reincarnates itself speaking to death and rebirth.

Solar consciousness refers to immortality, that which never dies. The moon reflects the sun's light because the consciousness of the sun keeps going and going. The reflection of the moon shuts on and off referring to direction. The sun rises in the East and sets in the West. This is important for people to understand because everything in terms of language is a personification. But there are two forms of consciousness, lunar and solar."

"Do you live in both worlds at the same time, two consciousness's at once?" she asks.

"You don't have to, although most of us do," he answers. "The problem is you know you have a conscience because you're aware through stepping back that you're thinking. That's disassociation. This proves you have a conscience."

"You can connect with your soul and draw solar light and soul energy into your cells, all the way to your atomic level, to activate more light within you and to accelerate your evolution.

Direction is important to understand in association with consciousness. Our consciousness has a directional mindscape. There is a north, south, east, and a west. It's unspoken, and a myriad of different thoughts coming from numerous directions. In terms of integration, the idea is getting just one thought from one direction to stand still. As a result you'll transcend yourself, integrating time and space. You become part and parcel of everything, which is how you achieve higher consciousness," St. Stephan reveals.

"How do you get that one thought to stand still?" she asks.

"The thought will stand still when you discover the secrets to manipulating direction," St. Stephan discloses. "Few people understand the direction of the mind, a reflection of the cosmos and cosmic consciousness. Try to think of one thing. Let's pretend you're thinking about a still pond in the beginning because you don't know if you're North, South,

East, West, Southwest, or Northeast. You simply don't know because you don't have a sense of it. This is why it's impossible to hold a thought still more than a few seconds. The first step in doing this leads you to the ability to transcend. Next is the first step in integration. It's about understanding direction and manipulating it mentally."

"Okay, I think I'm starting to understand," she says, scratching her head for a moment. "What happens when people who lack the ability to still their thoughts try to hold one thought still for a minute?"

"They don't know how to transcend time and space so they're almost immediately distracted with an interfering new thought," St. Stephan replies. "The thoughts overlap one another. Master the ability to hold one thought still and you'll be on your way to understanding 'The Mystery of Being'. It doesn't happen through many thoughts or through language, but through being. *Be the thought, just the one thought.* This will lead you down a path of spiritual integration."

"Where does God's Love come from, what part of our minds--North, South, East or West?" Sherilyn asks.

"Frank will tell you demons guard the various information in the cave, the things in the darkness, and those things dwell in the North," St. Stephan responds with laughter. "Break the rule and go north! Find the new information that resides in the North, bring it back, and tell people. Demons guard the information locked and preserved in the Chakras. However the demons don't know what they're guarding."

"How do you get past the demons?" She cross-examined.

St. Stephan replies, "Maneuver past the demons by going north. New information is in the North. You must go there personally as well to discover people who want to know. Sterling is already there in his mind and he brings back the new information.

Consider what I told both you and Sterling about Jesus being red and Mary being blue. You're already oriented in this, Sherilyn. You'll know what it means. Do you see Angie yet?"

"No, I need to get my directions straight and then I think I'll see her," she replies.

Place 33, Secrets of Universal Truths Revealed

"Okay, look to the Northeast," St. Stephan responds. "Angie is in the Northeast; Frank is in the Southwest and you know he's grumbling now.

He doesn't like the fact that she has new information. People can plug into it and actually accept the change; that's polarization."

"I'm curious, why do you always say look to the left?" Sherilyn asks.

"When you look to the left, you can change your perspective. I don't know why, but it's inevitable. Energy ebbs and flows, depending on how we want to characterize it. Energy doesn't stop its cyclical. That's why it can be understood and then manipulated.

Understanding structure relative to time and space is revealing. Structure exists between the interior relationships. It comes out of the connection of all parts creating a whole. Structure isn't context alone, but the content within the context. That's what structure is about."

"That's why there's a beginning, a middle, and an end," she says. "It feels like the gears are clicking into place."

"Yes," says St. Stephan. "So, mythological archetypes are valid. This notion of imagination being false or unreal is ridiculous. How people believe this is strange where do they think imagination comes from? Imagination is a bending, and maneuvering of the truth. A dramatization, actually."

"Changing the subject for a minute, is Sterling there with you now?" she asks St. Stephan, "Sterling's higher self."

"Sterling is back with you on Earth. Sterling is following me now," St. Stephan replies.

"Are you his lunar consciousness or his solar consciousness?" she asks.

"I'm simply Sterling's higher self," St. Stephan replied. "I'm the part of him that connects clearly into the collective consciousness, the universal consciousness, the pool of information that is to be accessed by a few, even though all of the people have the capacity to do it."

"Okay, I was just checking," she expresses.

"Returning to the value of direction, we must understand the limitations of language. There's no way man can understand 'The Mystery of Being'. Let's just call it Being. While in a state trapped between time and space, this must be transcended; then the truth is revealed. It's beyond thought, which is why it cannot be merely thought," St. Stephan emphasizes.

"I don't understand that yet," she says, shaking her head. St. Stephan states, "This sounds ridiculous at first. Providing people, who are open with an example of being still with one thought, will hopefully help them understand the revelation. It comes from the wisdom at the center of the four directions, which makes the tape spin. Each has a magnetic pull and so it elevates."

"How thick is it, this tape?" she inquired.

"Oh it is literally light years of depth. It's all the information, all the knowledge of humankind since the inception. Well, the tape has stopped now. I don't want to read anymore," Sterling relays lying on the couch.

"The original '3D Matrix' of separation and limitation is created and maintained by THOUGHTS of a polarized world, then fleshed out by the collective EMOTIONS of separation and limitation, and subsequently activated by the collective INTENTION for 'extreme individuality'.

A '5D Matrix' is created and maintained by THOUGHTS of Unity and ONENESS, EMOTIONS of Unconditional Love, Unconditional Acceptance, and Unconditional Forgiveness, and the INTENTION of Planetary Ascension.

Remember focus on the one thought. This will lead you down a path of spiritual integration."

"I feel like there is a very significant shift happening to the consciousness of the world and it's an exciting time to be here," she replies.

"Thank you for all your information. I love you Spiritual Father, St. Stephan," she says softly.

"I love my daughter," he says tenderly.

We end the hypnosis session

Place 33, Secrets of Universal Truths Revealed

Sherilyn Bridget Avalon

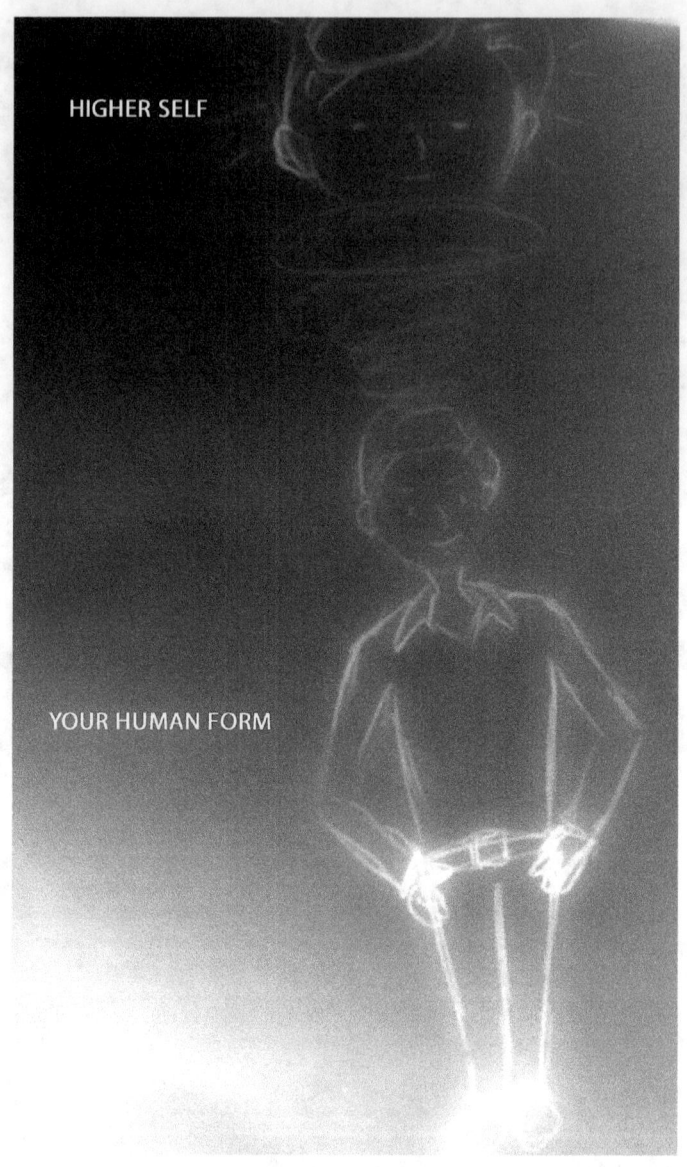

Place 33, Secrets of Universal Truths Revealed

Chapter 10 - Guardian of Egos

Later that evening Kenton and Sherilyn went out for dinner. He was stunning and reminded her of one of the men on the covers of romance novels. Kenton flashed a friendly smile and headed in her direction back from the Men's Room. She knew maintaining eye contact would be a struggle because she longed to bask in Kenton's arms, and be mesmerized by him for a few more minutes. The sexual energy between them began whispering to her. It was powerful and he was obviously trying to overtake her. Her earthly, physical impulses would love for Kenton to take her right then and there in his arms.

Mentally it was a battle, but one she was determined to win. What made the situation dangerous was she recognized Kenton felt this same sexual tension. She knew she could not allow these sexual thoughts to linger in her mind for another second, so she immediately changed her focus. She stopped. She had to play hard to get if she wanted him to be hers.

Kenton and Sherilyn pulled up to the hotel and parked. She opened her door, and started to climb out of the truck when Kenton appeared taking her hand and he helped her step down. Chivalrous to boot, she thought. Instead of Kenton, her thoughts returned to Sterling. She told Kenton "I have one child, a daughter." She didn't want to scare him away so early. She says, "Sterling, your janitor, wants to date me too."

"My janitor? No, Sterling's the elevator mechanic. It's been broke for a week. I haven't seen him at all. I've been trying to reach him. We keep missing each other, playing phone tag," Kenton relays. "If you see him, have him call me, please."

"Sure," Sherilyn responds, thinking it was strange he gave no response to her mentioning Sterling wanting to date her, "Thank you for dinner. I must be going now. It's about time to relieve the baby sitter."

"Wait, wait not so fast, how about a Magic Show on the Strip?" Kenton asks. "You can bring your daughter."

Place 33, Secrets of Universal Truths Revealed

"Yeah, that sounds fun. Call me," she says, making a sign of a phone with her hand to her ear and walks away toward her hotel room.

Sherilyn's cell phone is ringing as she walks in the room. It's Sterling calling. "I must see you," he says. Can you meet me at the wind tunnel?"

"Ahhh...Okay," she replies. He sounded like it was urgent. "How about you come over here," she replied. "I'm putting the kids to bed soon, so you can come around 9:00 tonight." She enjoys the Elevator with Sterling, too. She keeps discovering amazing bits and pieces about herself.

Sterling comes over and they jump in his car. As they are making their way to the Elevator of Enlightenment Sherilyn asked, "What's the big urgency?"

Sterling replies, "I feel St. Stephan. Since we have been doing these hypnosis sessions my connection with St. Stephan, my higher self is stronger. He is waiting for me on the other side of the elevator door patiently." He said, "A girl cries out!" Sterling acknowledges, "She's an old soul. She's between the Levels in the water. We need to find her! She's from the pool of knowledge."

"Really? You can hear people's thoughts in the pool of knowledge. How do you become an old soul?" Sherilyn asked. "Some of us are older than others, even though we're all created at the same time. Some of us didn't form till later on," Sterling` explains.

"Oh yeah? You said I was an old soul. Why didn't I get out of this misplacement if I'm so old?" Sherilyn asks him.

"Mmm-hmm. Yes, but you were cast into a dimension on earth that is more innocent than it should have been. Your knowledge was restricted and you made too many mistakes," he replied.

"That explains it," Sherilyn says sarcastically. Then she envisions Frank, the one in charge of all castings, deciding to flip the casting switch right before she was about to be cast into another dimension; and he double whammies her so she get double amnesia."

"Frank is disappointed because you're figuring him out," Sterling states.

"Oh really? Well, isn't that the name of the game? What are some other laws of the Universe?" she asks. As they are looking through the window at the Levels as they go by. Sherilyn asks, "What do you mean by form until later?"

St. Stephan continues, "The spirits of people who previously died stuck together. Somehow the people on Earth, alive at that time, realized it and managed to locate the knowledge."

"Oh, and I've always wondered about the pyramids in Egypt and why they were built. Can you see other information?" Sherilyn queried. "Were they built through hard work or levitation? How did they do it?"

St. Stephan explains, "They were highly inspired people who knew more than ordinary people know. They built the pyramids to draw energy. They drew energy proficiently and resourcefully. They also drew upon the pool of knowledge. It was a phenomenon on earth, an infinite thing.

They couldn't have done it without the inspiration of all those collective spirits of the people who were stuck together." St. Stephan says, "By burying the Egyptian Kings in pyramids it magnified their energy, thereby short-circuiting their stay."

"I see. Like when we die, do we immediately leave our bodies?" Sherilyn questioned.
St. Stephan states, "You have an attachment to your body for a while afterward. Most people don't want to think so, but it's true. If a body's cremated, there's no body remaining. Then there is no body for spirit to remain attached to, but there's

honestly no 'best way' to do it." Sterling and Sherilyn continue looking at each other in the elevator. Sterling is acting a little strange.

Sherilyn asks, "Sterling, how are you? What do you see out the elevator window?"

"Light, but its not really light; its gold like a sunburst medallion. I'm just looking at it through the window. Let me

Place 33, Secrets of Universal Truths Revealed

look. I see it now. It's a medallion on a pedestal. It sits. It's sitting where the lily pads usually are," Sterling commented.

"Are there lily pads there?" Sherilyn asks.

"Let me see," Sterling says, as he moves toward the window of the elevator. "Oh yeah, but the medallion is taking up almost all of the space; it's taken up most of the horizon. It's huge!"

"But what is it for?" Sherilyn asks.

"I'm not quite sure," Sterling ponders, "it's more like who is it for?" He pauses a moment. "It's for my knowledge. I don't know why it's so big." He exclaims.

"Then who gave it to you?" Sherilyn asks.

"It's a gift from Angie, "Sterling says smiling. "Yes, it's a gift for my knowledge. It has many petals, like clovers, clover petals."

"It looks like a clover? Is it a four leaf clover?" Sherilyn inquired.

He starts counting, "1, 2, 3, 4, 5, 6, 7, 8, 9, nine leaf clover. It's very bright and beautiful and behind it is pure white light; it's quite large."

"Does it say anything on it, any important information? What does it say?" Sherilyn questioned.

Sterling responds, "Well, it's full of information. It's not on the face but it's obviously a significant object. It looks like it's the place where the gold tape is stored. But it appears that it's more than one gold tape; it appears that there are many."

"And this is where they are stored?" Sherilyn asked.

He looks closely at the clover. "I can't see that; it just seems for that to be the case," Sterling answers.

"Is it a storage place for the tapes?" Sherilyn questions.

"That's what it seems; I don't know why it's here. I'm looking at it now. I think I'll get out and really stand next to the clover. Would you like to come with me?" Sterling asks.

"Yes, "Sherilyn replies curiously. "I'm with you."

"I like to watch you look at the giant medallion. You look like an ant (they laugh) so do I. Well I guess I look more like a grasshopper," Sterling replies, "just size wise, compared to the medallion. It's really large. It's unbelievably, absolutely beautiful, but the white light shining through its clover is very meaningful. I can see that. And of course Angie's small now. She's not usually that small; it's just because there's so much space taken up with the medallion that she's smaller. And to the bottom right Frank is crouching as usual. I think I'll start to climb up the medallion. It looks inviting." Sterling comments.

"Is it like a coin serrated on the side?" Sherilyn asks.

"No, it's just like a medallion with the shape of the clover leafs, nine of them. It is so interesting. Okay. The ninth leaf has the number 18 inscribed on it."

"What does that mean?" Sherilyn questions.

"I think it means that it's an entrance to level 18. It has something to do with level 18 and it's very old." Sterling replies quizzically.

"Is it Celtic?" Sherilyn asked.

"Let me look. Come up here with me," Sterling requests. He reaches his arm down toward Sherilyn to pull her onto this pedestal.

"Wow! It's so large!" Sherilyn comments.

The 9th leaf has an inscription on it, number 18. There's pollen coming out when you open the door. Yeah, it looks like gold dust. It's funny feeling, it's fuzzy, it sticks to you, and it feels like it's telling me something," Sterling replies.

"What?" Sherilyn exclaims.

"Okay. Frank said this is the pollen of my personal ego and that I should go and saturate myself with it, that I should collect it up, then put it in the urn, and then drink it, even though it's a kind of sticky dust. By doing so I will be able to reveal my ego to myself, as I am detached from it and view it for what it is.

So, there's more. He says that if I do this, that I would also be able to view your ego as well, as we hold hands and you can drink along with me," Sterling explained.

"Okay! This is so strange." She says, "First we take the urns and leave the medallion?" Sherilyn questioned. That didn't sound right.

Place 33, Secrets of Universal Truths Revealed

"Frank says, 'to take off the leaf', and use it as a pedestal, and go up to Level 18. Get out and sit down on it," Sterling relays.

"Okay let's do that," Sherilyn says with enthusiasm.

"It's so light, I can't believe it. Carrying the leaf is like being an ant. They can carry more than their weight. An ant can carry this huge thing around; it's so light, like carrying nothing at all. It's really something, God! Okay, let's get back in the elevator." Sterling commands crisply.

"Frank seems to be liking this but he's not smiling and Angie says it's okay. So let's just do it. We're back into the elevator. I have a hold of it. You can grab it. Grab a hold of it with me. That's good! Hold it down; have it merge with yourself. It's almost like touching nothing.

We're in the elevator. Now let's go on up, push the button to 18. 'Oh my God!' It just turned the entire interior brilliant gold! Were kicking around Gold dust, Jesus, it's like kicking the truth around. Man it must be at least 3 feet deep. This stuff is really cool. 'God it's sticky!' But it doesn't quite stick to you. It's like powdery snow. Are you kicking it with me? It's so light it feels like nothing; it's lighter then ash." Sterling comments.

"It's like powdered snow?" Sherilyn repeats.

"Okay let's just open the door," Sterling commands.

"We're at level 18. The doors are opening," Sherilyn directs.

"Oh, I see Frank. He's beckoning us with two hands. He's beckoning us; both of his hands are outstretched, index and middle finger up, palms up, and he's motioning for us to come near. He says make sure that you gather up all the dust."

"Okay did we get it all?" Sherilyn comments.

Angie is just watching.

"Wow!" Sterling exclaims. "It's a gold trail with a white light background.

Frank looks flesh like, in his brown skin suit, and his blue eyes, and he's motioning us with his two fingers.

Okay, just take my hand; we'll follow Frank. Now it's configured itself right back, just like the way it was, and is taking up two-thirds of the sky again. It's so immense."

"But, we just had it in the elevator," Sherilyn giggles.

Frank says, "be still, and I'll reveal some things to you through the gold." Sterling starts moaning as Frank is showing him things.

Sherilyn is asking Angie "Is it okay to speak with Frank here?" Angie says, "it's okay to speak with Frank anywhere." Sherilyn says, "okay."

"Okay Frank we're in a new element here. What's up?" Sterling asks.

Frank says, "It's not really gold, you know, it just looks like it is"

Sherilyn asks, "Well, what is it?"

"It's what Sterling's ego looks like, when you're able to view it when you are outside of yourself," Frank replies.

Sterling quizzically says, "It's funny that it looks like gold. Does everyone's ego look like this Frank?"

Frank says, "No, everyone's does not," in a matter of fact kind of way.

Sterling says, "Is everyone's ego as light as this Frank?"

Frank replies, "No, they vary widely in terms of the density."

"Why are you allowing me to look at it Frank?" Sterling asks.

"Because it will help you to understand why you have it, and it will help you to understand why yours is lighter, and why yours is larger, and why yours is golden," Frank replies.

"Angie wants to know if you would like to know what your ego looks like Sherilyn." Sterling questions.

"Well, yes, I would," she replies sheepishly.

"Angie wants to know if you can see her." Sterling queried.

"No, I can't right now. It's dark," Sherilyn replies sadly. "I'm not able to see her because I have not meditated enough to get the connection to the other side that you need," Sherilyn responds.

"Angie's disappointed! Sterling says. "She says that she will show it to you anyway and that you can use Sterling as a conduit for your eyes."

Place 33, Secrets of Universal Truths Revealed

"Okay! That would be awesome!" Sherilyn excitedly agrees.

Angie says, "You need to trust in Sterling's ability to convey, so you can see."

"I do!" Sherilyn says with heartfelt appreciation.

"I see it forming," Sterling laughs. (They both laugh.) Sterling starts to convey, "It looks quite different than mine does. Its nice looking, I like it! It's ivory in color, it's a lot denser, and it's thicker. It looks like…can you see it? It's growing right out of the top of your head and configuring. It's like a large cloverleaf shaped balloon. It is almost like an aura but it's an appendage from your head. It's very dense compared to what I'm looking at; and there's no pattern to it. It's not shedding anything like mine, which is shedding all over the place."

"Are you shedding your ego honey?" Sherilyn kids with him.

"I have a lot of powder coming off of mine. Yours is ivory, and its heavy. It almost looks burdensome; it's weighted. Let me touch it once," he says.

"What does it feel like?" Sherilyn asks with the excitement of discovering her ego for the first time. "Not that it's a good thing, or is it?"

Sterling proceeds to touch it. "It looks neat?"

He says, as he proceeds to examine it as if holding a magnifying glass.

Sherilyn asks the question, "Does it look like a clover?" wanting it to be like Sterling's."

"Yeah," Sterling says with hesitation.

"How many leafs?" she asks.

"Just the one!" he says quietly.

"Oh yeah," Sherilyn says disappointedly.

Sterling communicates, "You only have one, but actually it's better; you don't want a big ego. The ego's job is to give us anxiety about the past and fear about the future. Let's touch it once," Sterling chuckles. "Oh my God! It looks hard but it feels gooey. It's so strange! I can't believe that we can actually look at the structure of an ego. It is amazing."

"Is it?" Sherilyn interjects, being coy.

"Christ, no wonder they're such a burden. Man yours is really heavy! Damn! Angie wants you to see it. That is such a strange site," Sterling comments.

"Really, how big is it?" hoping it's not as big as his.

"Oh, it's huge!" Sterling blurts out.

"Bigger than yours?" Sherilyn asks with hint of disappointment.

"No," Sterling says reluctantly.

"I didn't think so! Is it half the size of yours? Sherilyn was trying to figure the comparison."

"No, it is just denser. It's maybe a third less in size; maybe, that's it. Can't you see? But of course, it looks hard, but it's not shedding anything. That's really quite revealing somehow. "

"Oh my god!" Sterling is shocked. There's something coming in the sky... It has taken on a blue hue. There…in between where our two clovers don't quite meet. It's taking on a blue hue but, the rest of the sky is white."

"What does that mean?" Sherilyn asks, confused in not being able to see the egos because she wasn't quite ready.

"I could tell you it's someone else's ego, not ours." Sterling surmises.

"Uh, oh! Who?" Sherilyn asks, shocked.

Angie says, "This is the place where Egos are revealed."

"It's someone else's ego," Sterling relays, intrigued.

"Are we still on Level 18?" Sherilyn reiterated.

Sterling replies, "No, actually it's nine, but we have to view the ego through the combination of the one and the eight." Angie relays, "because otherwise we wouldn't really be able to see what we're seeing, because it would be transparent."

"The only way to make it not transparent would be to divide it. In other words divide nine into one and eight. Because that way we will be able to see the two halves and they will present. And if it was just singular we wouldn't be able to see it." Sterling interprets.

Angie relays, "Someone who has died is about to speak with us?"

Place 33, Secrets of Universal Truths Revealed

"Who?" Sherilyn asked.

"This person is going to have a large effect upon Sterling's thinking," Angie telepathically relays, "This will also be very revealing to Sherilyn. It will be very important to incorporate this person's conveyance under hypnosis to what we are in the process of attempting to do in terms of the information you can put in the book."

"Okay," Sherilyn replies.

"This man likes the conveyance of information, and this man also likes Sterling," Angie relays.

"Who is this man?" Sherilyn asks intriguingly.

"He says, that his name is Joseph," Angie relayed.

"Joseph Campbell?" Sherilyn questions. She intuitively feels it to be him.

"Oh my God he's dead! " (Sterling breathing hard)

"It's ok honey!" Sherilyn tries to calm him down.

"The presence is peering in. He wants to speak. He says he has unfinished business," Sterling speaks unsure.

"It's okay to let him pass through you," Sherilyn reassures him. "Does he feel like a good spirit? Then let him pass through you, people do it all the time. Its called channeling"

He says, "that I'm molecularly light," Sterling conveys. "Even though I have a large ego, its quite movable. He feels I'm a useful subject in this form and he would be interested in conveying information because he was only capable of making the transition two-thirds of the way to the light. And it's going to be relatively easy for him to make a complete transition only after he is able to divest himself from his incomplete lesson. He gave into pain."

"Oh yeah! Who is he?" Sherilyn pleads.

Sterling answers, "His name is Joseph, as he's part of the fabric that makes up the composite of what Josephs are."

"Okay, well let him speak," says Sherilyn.

Sterling says, "If I will allow it, participate and help, that even though it will make me uncomfortable, I will become a wiser person on earth with my ego, and I will deal with it in a more constructive manner."

Joseph says," If I use you, Sherilyn, in a proper manner, I will be able to succeed in conveying the last third of my lesson to others."

"That is what has prevented him from completing his transition." Sterling relays.

"Ok...wow!" Sherilyn is in shock. (She didn't think this could happen through hypnosis). She feels this is a lot to put on a person.

Sterling expresses, "He is very pleased with this opportunity that somehow he has managed to open up through our two egos. He says, you don't know me, but that I am very close to the same level of consciousness that St. Stephan is."

"Oh!" Sherilyn replies. "Sterling's higher self?"

Joseph says, "That's why most folks find Sterling complicated. But with my help, Sterling will be a more influential conveyor."

"That's good!" Sherilyn reiterates.

Then Sterling confides, "He will appreciate this a great deal because he will have completed what he was meant to do."

"That will be helping him; that will be good. Do you want to do it?" Sherilyn quizzes Sterling.

"Yes," Sterling replies emphatically.

"Great!" says Joseph. Joseph is extremely happy.

"Oh boy, he's got a long *tape. Jesus, its wound tight; it's wound long. It's wide and it's trailing behind his head," says Sterling.

"Really?" Sherilyn says with amazement.

"He's anxious, if that's the correct word, to complete what he wanted to say in body. But his body gave out and he's now sorry that he gave in to the pain. He says that I handle pain better than he does." Sterling boasts.

"Yes, you handle pain pretty well," Sherilyn, affirmed.

"He wants to tell you that the reason your ego is Ivory is because it represents the carrot of purity, and you're tainted; and your lesson is to learn how to become untainted," says Sterling.

Place 33, Secrets of Universal Truths Revealed

"Okay, I'm listening intently now," says Sherilyn.

"He's telling me, that my ego is gold because it carries the blessing of wisdom, and that the carrot for me is that I'm close to losing it, and that is why it is so light," Sterling relays.

"That's really good." Sherilyn looks at Sterling with admiration.

"He knows... This individual knows a lot." Sterling is breathing hard. "This man has lived a very intricate matrix of lives. ...Much information, many pathways, but couldn't tolerate the pain. He gave up and now he regrets it and is being allowed this opportunity to say more.

He says that in the months to come, if I will allow him to help, there will be much more forthcoming information that will be very clear and very helpful to everyone that hears it."

"Okay. Are we supposed to help any particular person?" Sherilyn asks.

Angie says, "Sterling helps most people he deals with and that he is old and well-intentioned. He is particularly useful in that he manages pain fairly well, for a sensitive individual that has the kind of sensitivity that is required to know this much and be this clear of a conveyor." She says, "It is a unique combination of abilities."

Sterling states, "Angie wants you back; and you, she says, have been faltering; you have been giving into your ego. You have become petty of late, and she is rather disappointed." She says, "Your problems will cease to exist with men if you learn the lesson of lightening your ego. The Ivory texture of your ego and the weighted mass of it, will become much less molecularly weighted once you stop being so resentful with your lesson that you're learning through men."

"Okay Angie. I understand," says Sherilyn. Even though she really didn't understand the lessons or why she had to go through these lessons. (Marriage to a man old enough to be her father, molested at 13, date raped twice, once by a director, losing children, etc.)

Sterling turned to Sherilyn, "Joseph is listening and watching, and it seems that he has always been the part of energy that represents curiosity."

"Yes, that's right!" Joseph restated.

"That's Joseph, the personification of curiosity," St. Stephan responds.

Frank says, "I want the information to be perfected and I want the process to take a long time."

Angie says, "If Sherilyn can learn how to stop being so personal with her agitation with Sterling's ego, that will not be necessary."

Joseph is simply watching this as if at a theater, as if he's ready to eat another piece of popcorn. He is enjoying himself immensely and he feels very good to have the opportunity now; this is what he has hoped for. He is an extremely emanating entity.

"This person was personified knowledge on earth. He was practically a vortex for it because of the manner in which he developed structurally in terms of his mind. He seems to be too focused though, through his perfectionistic flaw on detail. I can see this now; I am looking at his mind," says St. Stephan.

"It's funny, it's like looking through a magnifying glass; it is all becoming clearer now. I can't see his face anymore," Sterling articulates.

"What does he look like?" Sherilyn coaxes him.

"He's kind of got bushy eyebrows and rather prominent lines running down his face on each side of the nose, and has a rather anxious but gentle look about him--kind of like you. He just can't get enough done," Sterling replies.

"Part of that seems to be that for all of his wisdom--from being a presenter of unifying concepts in comparative mythology--all of his explaining, all of the benefits, had resulted in him being stifled by his own personal defeat in not being able to handle his pain," Sterling analyzes.

"What was his last name?" Sherilyn looks intensely into Sterling's eyes. "Say it! Just say it!"

"Well, he has had many last names, but this particular personification was named after the soup...Campbell Soup. Red label, and it appears that minestrone and tomato was his favorite as a child," Sterling says so straightforwardly.

"Oh yeah?" Sherilyn chuckles.

Place 33, Secrets of Universal Truths Revealed

"He didn't like bean and bacon!" Sterling recaps.

"Joseph Campbell, yeah I know who he is. That's what I thought! He was quite an admired man on Earth. He wrote the book 'Man & Myth,'" Sherilyn recalls.

"Whew! He is firm in his intent and his confidence, that Sterling can pick up where he left off, which is intimidating Sterling's ego," Angie's relaying to Sherilyn. She has to drop her façade, her shell, and her heaviness, that she understands what to do, yet can't do it.

Angie is disappointed. Frank is not.

"I'm sorry Angie! I guess I'm just too personal. I just want to be left alone for a while," Sherilyn speaks louder.

Sterling says, "Joseph was going to do something under hypnosis and then his ego got in the way."

Frank says to Sherilyn, "Well what else can you expect."

Sterling tells me. Angie says, "This is a test of your own tolerance and wisdom, and that you're not really making a very high-grade," Sherilyn laughs, and then bows her head.

"You have met someone that is truly exceptional," Angie relays. "If you will simply allow yourself, through the wisdom that you already have, to be the vessel of your own wisdom, quite an impact of impression will occur. It will almost be like a starburst. It really does hinge upon you and how you deal with Sterling. Because, Sterling has a sensitivity to rejection and he feels hurt that you are uncomfortable with being close and he tries so hard, to the maximum of his own sphere relative to his ego interest."

"He always expects something in return; that's what I don't like," Sherilyn added.

St. Stephan interjects, "All egos expect returns. This is part and parcel of dealing with the physical world that exists, given this particular juncture in time that all of you are dealing with."

Angie says, "You need to be stiller, calmer so that you can implement more of what you know, so you can leave your ego aside. It is stifling you and your efforts."

"Meditation?" Sherilyn asks.

Frank says, "Reject Sterling's love; you will learn more."

"Is it true Angie?" Sherilyn asks.

Angie says, "I refuse to dignify Frank's attitude with a response."

"I just don't know. I'll try to be more still." Sherilyn says.

As Sterling stares at Joseph, and says with a quivery lip, "I can't believe this…this man, his intent…it's too strong. I've never felt anyone with such unfinished business; I'm having goose bumps in my mind."

"The energy is strong, but he is not as large as I am, St. Stephan integrates. That made him anxious too, and that's also why he couldn't handle his pain as well." St. Stephan bellows, "Sterling will help."

"Of course!" Sterling replies.

Joseph is very appreciative. Joseph comments, "There will be many more meetings to come.

It's the unison of the energy that Sherilyn and Sterling bring that will result in synergy, *if they are capable of meeting the challenge of the separation of the ego."*

"This is very wise energy," Sterling recites to Sherilyn.

"Thank you Joseph," Sherilyn replied.

Sterling still staring at the sky, "This is so strange he's not quite dead. I've never experienced this before; I'm uncomfortable with it. It's okay; it's just so different," Sterling's emotions going back and forth like a gyroscope.

"Does he look young or old?" Sherilyn asks Sterling.

"Older, yes, definitely," Sterling replied.

"Don't you go back to like, 30 - 35 when you die?" Sherilyn heard that somewhere.

"No! He's not dead. He's not complete! He's stuck! He's stuck!" Sterling says with deep emotions.

"Oh! I see he's stuck like that one, Spirit we set free. Does he still have emotions attached to his body, or I mean attached to the world?" Sherilyn asks.

"It's sticky you know? He has things to convey." Sterling replies.

"Unfinished business to complete? Okay what level is he on?" Sherilyn asked.

Place 33, Secrets of Universal Truths Revealed

"I met him right here. It's not really on a level. He's in between things; things aren't delineated. He's grappling, looking, searching. He couldn't meet the one challenge. Sterling shakes his head. "Too bad!"

"What did he have, cancer? That's a hard painful lesson." Sherilyn says with empathy.

"He had other things too. He just grew old. He also had emphysema, blocked arteries that were degenerating, and he also had psychological fear. It gave him this obsession," St. Stephan explains to Sherilyn.

"As you realize by now, progress entails pain. For me it's not as much physical as it is emotional pain. That is the way progress is structured, until it changes. You should take advantage of it. I can draw from Angie. She is still; she is pure but Frank is trying to confuse you," St. Stephan adds. "He's trying to make you into a self-centered individual.

He's playing on your ego's weaknesses, given your brainwashed past in this lifetime and others, disallowing you from being as clear, as calm, and as passive as you can be Sherilyn. If you are passive with males, they will be passive with you."

"You are blind. You are blind by design, because Frank wants you not to see. He wants you to feel the pain of disappointment, the pain of confusion, the pain of redundancy. Ego is nature's way of teaching you saturation. Step out of your ego. Operate with passivity, enlightenment, charisma and you will walk among the Masters," Joseph imparts to Sherilyn.

"I will?" Sherilyn answers in shock. "Wow! I can learn a lot about the other side and LIFE from Joseph. I can hardly believe it. I am going to be facilitating the channeling of Joseph Campbell's previous life. L.I.F.E. is… Living In Frequency Earth."

Sherilyn Bridget Avalon

Chapter 11 – Mystery of Being

Sherilyn goes back to Phoenix to see her Therapist. Sherilyn explains her adventures to her Therapist, "So we run into the entity named Joseph Campbell as he is trying to complete his quest for transcendence. Every time we run into him he relays a little more of his experiences on the other side. Can you hypnotize me and let's see if we can contact him? Because I would like to see him."

Her Therapists puts Sherilyn under hypnosis and this is what she says, "Joseph sits on a log. He lost his foot. He practically falls off his log as we come into The Place through the elevator of enlightenment. We greet each other and its like we never left."

"Hi Joseph," Sherilyn greets him. "We are looking for a female thought that is lost in the pool of knowledge."

"I did see a lost soul on Level 7," Joseph comments. " But, I really want to explain what I have been learning," as he is eager to get started with his essay.

He says, "Earth isn't much different from where I'm at now. You don't see with your eyes; you don't hear with your ears. You feel it in a much more in-depth, crisp, ultra reality. When the universe began, life emerged through a process that was the antithesis of the big bang theory.

The fragments of energy were millions and billions of times smaller than a cell's nucleus. Extremely infinitesimal, self-feeding, and self-expanding particles started the phenomenon.

Without time, there is no space. Without space there is no time, and there's a boundary to it. Eventually it expands beyond its saturation point. Then it recoils and mass will stick together again. Finally it will return back to that fragment of energy and then we start all over again." Joseph explains, "All of life is sorrowful. You have misplaced qualities in your sphere. You're what I call a Femanale Being. When you're calm you attract, when you're aggressive you repel."

"Its nice to meet you too Joseph!" Sherilyn says sarcastically in love, knowing that there are no secrets here; all is revealed.

Angie likes Joseph. She says, "He is at the pinnacle of his sphere. Joseph's sphere is dawn-like."

"Joseph wants us to know that eternity is not something coming in the future. It's in the here and now," Joseph relays to Sherilyn.

Joseph continues, "If you can, put your mind in a transcendental thought state, a Nirvana State. God is a thought, an Idea. The reference to God speaks beyond the parameters or boundaries of thought. That's a transcended place.

Beyond space and time this field is only one that's experienced, not defined. It dwells within us and without, when you find it. You'll find the field of opposites made of male and female polarity. They take on form and you perceive, giving each person the life they're living. For example: the field is magnetic and near the tree of illumination.

The best things in life are matters that can't be described or written. It's impossible to try and explain it, just experience it. When you go to the field, make sure you understand how a trilogy works. Situate your mind directly in-between the pair of opposites."

"Oh yeah, that's cool," Sherilyn says.

"When you go to the field, this is how you must explore it," Joseph relays. "We're on Level Seven, the place of mysteries revealed. What do you see Sherilyn?" Joseph asks, watching him from his log perch.

"Look to the Left!" Sherilyn says, as she giggles. "It looks like a Z, but it's a 7. What is it?"

"Its the base of the seven." Joseph replies. "The bottom of the level looks like a line because it's so flat, which makes it look like a 'Z'. The seven represents mysteries revealed. That's why it gained the reputation for being so lucky. It's a very important place," he relays.

"When going through the seven, you go along the bottom and go up the tunnel; travel up to the first bend, then take a left,

Place 33, Secrets of Universal Truths Revealed

and then wind up at the end of the left line on the top. It's like a bubble at the end. You are at the end of it, or the beginning, depending on your perspective. "It's very abstract here, very magical, the birthplace of the number seven," Joseph interjects.

"Numbers are born?" Sherilyn questioned, perplexed.

"Metaphors, metaphors for different types of movement," Joseph replies. "Math is actually quite abstract. It just looks like it's not."

"Feel how elastic it is. I have never explored this part of the left. It's different; there is so much to see here. It has an interesting hairy kind of fiber look to it. It's kind of fuzzy. It's quite dramatic in the way that it looks; it's really light, kind of bluish green, very clear. It's white with a bluish green cast on it," Joseph replies.

Here comes a Mystery: "I see the lost girl. Her name is Jane and she's with some children. They all died of AIDS. That's what they're saying. I'm in a barrel or maybe a cavern. Yes, in the cavern you can see the fish," Joseph revealed.

Just then we flashback in our minds to the Therapist office in 3D on the Earth.

"The fish?" The Therapist replied.

Sherilyn started speaking, "Yes, they're fish in Africa. There are larvae in the river and in the fish, the blind fish. They're blind from disease. Mostly they're found in carp, a scavenger fish in Africa. No one would ever think of it. The vaccine to cure the disease is in the worm, the larvae. Researchers can do it. Scientists don't believe it yet, but it is true. The cure, a live vaccine, is in the larvae. Jane said it was, and she died of AIDS. She knows the truth!"

"What river in Africa?" asked the Therapist.

"It starts with a 'G'", Sherilyn replies, "sounds like GA-gan-chi, or Ganchi River in North Sudan; the river leads out of the country. It sounds like that." Umm, Sherilyn tries to remember, but isn't sure.

"Or maybe Gambi River; the river leads out of the country. Scientists could develop the vaccine very cost-effectively. It's so obvious--the cure to AIDS can be found in a small-polluted river in Sudan. Let's ask Angie and Frank if it's true. Then onward to Level 33."

Sherilyn explains to the Therapist, St. Stephan decides to join us. "We are sitting on this lily pad at The Place on Level 33, getting filled with the water. Our feet are dangling in the clear, white water as we look at the spheres of energy floating around us."

St. Stephan says, "Rivers are the arteries of our planet. The steady flow of clean fresh water is an essential element for vast ecosystems and the health and survival of billions of people."

"Yes! I believe that," the Therapist interjects.

Sherilyn's asking St. Stephan about her friend Louise who just crossed over. She had AIDS, too. "How is my friend Louise doing?" Sherilyn asks Joseph.

"Do you see her? Can you communicate with her?" the Therapist asks.

"Yes, because she's hoping she'll meet someone from the same sphere as Sterling when she returns.

"Why is that?" Asks the Therapist?

"Louise is very pleased. She's peering in one face of three. Her face appears vibrantly alive; it looks the same as it did before she was truly sick with AIDS." Joseph reports to Sherilyn, "She looks over you. She passionately wants to be seen. This will continue another three to five weeks. She has to visit half again past the 13th hour."

"What do you mean 'one face of three?'" the Therapist asked. Sherilyn replied. "I noticed this face in my room last night. I was going to mention that to you. I mentioned it to St. Stephan."

St. Stephan said, "She's pleased you've found a guidepost, a guiding light. She watches with interest now. Only the face of Louise is left.

There's a line between the spaces, which allows her to see two levels--half again beyond the 13th hour, which is where she'll find the other two thirds of herself."

"Why are there three faces?" the Therapist asks.

Sherilyn replies; Joseph says, "The third face is the one she sees through forgiveness. Without the third face, she couldn't see into what she lived through. She needs to fill herself up completely with the emotions left from her life that lives in the people she left behind.

Once she's absorbed the reflection of the emotions that she left in them, and she's connected to them, then she'll finally complete her transition. This will happen in five weeks, and it will be half again past the 13th hour. She looks with intent. She's completely happy to be free from her body."

"Yeah, I bet she is." Sherilyn exclaimed. "She was in so much pain with that horrible AIDS."

"Louise likes Sterling very much. She isn't jealous of you. She's always content for you. After she reached saturation, she became happy. A level of pain allowed her to look on things from her forgiven face." Joseph added.

"Is she a forgiven soul?" the Therapist asks.

"Now she's forgiven. St. Stephan told me this," Sherilyn replied.

"She wasn't before?" the Therapist queried.

Sherilyn explains, "Next time when she comes back she'll be forgiven. When she does, she'll choose with a forgiven mindset. It's in between Level 13 and 14. When she finds her other 'two thirds' of herself, then her three faces will be whole. She'll start over in a manner that will be less painful and more enlightened. Louise will eventually have a life with someone who'll remind her of boyfriend Tom. She's glad she taught Tom (her boyfriend) what he needed," Sherilyn rambles on. "Tom is saturated with pain. He's experiencing emotional torture from the loss, knowing he will never speak to Louise again, the one whom he came to love so very much. This is what she says in her own way, without moving her lips."

"Do you see her face?" asks the Therapist.

"I did, in my room, I saw this pink energy with three faces. I don't anymore," Sherilyn said, wishing she could see Louise once more. "There's not a lot left. She has a glowing white face with a pink hue, blue eyes that are deep set now. Otherwise it looks like her. She has no illness here.

"Sounds like an orb to me," replied the Therapist.

Sherilyn interjects; Louise asked me, "Why I don't feel more remorseful when people pass on?"

I answered her question; "I'm not sure Louise. I guess it's because I believe you're in a better place now. Should I feel more remorse? You're finally out of your pain from AIDS. I doubt it would be better for you here," Sherilyn trails on.

"Louise said, 'You hide your emotions in glass tubes.'

Joseph relays, "It appears that way as she looks at you from her dimension. She thinks you should empty the tubes and dispose of them. She says, "Do that and you'll have a more free correlation between your feelings, what you know, and your experiences."

"My reaction confuses her because she doesn't know me that well." I tell the Therapist.

"She watches over her family. For three more weeks; then her faces will integrate. At that point she'll be a whole person who has transmuted. When she returns it'll be on a higher level of consciousness," Sherilyn explains to the therapist. "I impart to Louise, I'm sorry you had to go through so much pain, with genuine sadness this time."

"Louise says, you should cry more Sherilyn," Joseph relays. "She was allowed to look at the red tape, and she hopes one day to gaze at the gold tape," Sherilyn tells the Therapist.

"Oh really! What's on the red tape?" the Therapist asks. Sherilyn explains; Joseph says, "The red tape stores information of orientation by fire. There's a level of great understanding about instinct and the wisdom that arises from the understanding of instinct. This is in contrast to other types of understanding, which are transcendent or divine beyond the realm of nature for those who have the privilege of, or good fortune as Louise calls it, to view the Gold Tape. The gold tape stores information from the inception of man. Viewing the Gold Tape is an experience she passionately wants. However, that's not exactly how it works. One has to be at a higher consciousness to view it.

Louise had a message for Tom?" Sherilyn explained.

"She says, 'things aren't always as they appear.' She says that Love really can be a very enlightening thing. It doesn't have to involve reciprocation in the way that he had previously thought. She hopes Tom realizes her love for him will always live. It will remain in his mind until he dies and transmutes himself. Because it's real," St. Stephan said, "this should comfort him."

"As long as the thought stays alive she'll be alive in fragments with him and anyone else who remembers her. It's like sprinkling water on flowers. The thought of the person is the flower, and the energy coming from the mind that's crossed over is the water. The interaction is in the living person's subconscious mind. She's done a good job and she suffered a great deal. Every pore of her body was pain-filled." Joseph says.

"That sounds like what my Biological Father said when he did that contest about the soul." Sherilyn says, It's terrible, the pain, wincing in empathy for her friend.

St. Stephan explained to me what Louise telepathically relayed. "She thinks you should be careful. If you don't stop hiding your feelings and get in touch with them, you won't meet the challenge of your true potential. You'll have to come back and live it all over again."

"She can see this?" the Therapist probes.

Sherilyn replied, "well, St. Stephan explained it to me. She can't see all parts of me, not totally. There's one-third of me she doesn't see. Louise has good intent, however.

"I told Louise I appreciated her, and thanked her," Sherilyn replied. "I am trying to empty my glass tubes. I am facing a lot of emotional pain, like she suffered through physical pain."

Then St. Stephan said, "Yes, let's move forward now. Louise is fine, Louise is in no danger, and she learned her lesson. Frank is smiling and Angie says it is okay. Next time it won't be so grueling for her."

"I am relieved," says Sherilyn. "Knowing how much pain Louise suffered with AIDS is difficult, but I am glad the lesson is complete."

Then St. Stephan says, "Let's go to the place Louise inadvertently commented upon. Let's climb back into the elevator and off we go."

We say our goodbyes to Louise tell her we love her. "Ask if she can come with us?"

St. Stephan says, "She can hear from her perspective and see through her face," he replied. "Let's go back to Level 28 for a second. Let's get in the mist; I want you to breathe in the green mist for a while. If you aren't from a higher level of consciousness you can't go there. Her vibration couldn't take it."

We're at Level 28 and the door whooshes open. We both inhale deeply a whiff of the green mist. Mmm-hmmm, refreshing chlorophyll, like freshly cut grass.

"Don't talk, just breathe it in," St. Stephan says.

"Hey, Joseph do you want to come with us to Level 13 and one half? Can he come?" Sherilyn asks St. Stephan. Because St. Stephan is very indulgent with his daughter, he nods "yes" allowing her to have her whims, and we bring Joseph along and Louise listens.

Then St. Stephan said, "We need to understand how saturation works. I know no matter how much an individual contemplates; it doesn't detract from his beingness. The individual is so malleable; no fragment belonging to him is ever lost. It always returns. Joseph, unfortunately, doesn't enjoy that degree of security. That's why he's stuck; he didn't trust enough in his own wisdom and genius. He allowed pain and fear to overwhelm his judgment. Faith is a pivotal thing. We create our own reality. What you believe is where you live and we all live in our minds.

If you believe, you can be strong enough to allow people to take bits and pieces from you and run away from you. They can run hundreds, thousands of miles away. Eventually, the strength of your gravitational pull will ultimately lead you to become whole again. When you have peace of mind deep within, nothing will defeat you.

It doesn't matter how many pieces you're broken into, you know eventually you'll be whole again. That kind of belief is undefeatable."

We were traveling through some kind of green mist. We're filled with the water from the mist now, refreshed, clear and ready to see something different, because we haven't been there before.

St. Stephan relayed, "Okay, we're here. We're at Level 13 and one half. It's an interesting Place. Franks here!" he declares.

"Why is it 13 and one half?" The Therapist interjects.

Place 33, Secrets of Universal Truths Revealed

"Let me ask St. Stephan," Sherilyn says.

St. Stephan replied, "Because this is where time stops. There's a balance as it moves diametrically forward and backwards. Therefore, there's no time on this level. Time doesn't move ahead nor does it move backward. In an odd twist, it moves equally in both directions at the same time.

It's not just the 13th hour but also half past the 13th hour. The margin of error lives here on this Level."

Frank walks into the room; of course he's naked. "Take a good look Joseph, this is where you went off. The origin of Physics resides on this Level. The roots are embedded in the stillness. The margin of error is an integration of time and space. All half Levels are futuristic ones like this. They deal primarily with the lines between the spaces. We can see incredibly complex spheres of energy once we get inside. The complexity leads us first to Physics — a physical manifestation of the spirit. In your world's time only Metaphysicians understood this notion," Frank comments.

"What is Physics? Mathematics or Calculus?" Sherilyn asks Frank.

"Physics has its roots here at the Level of the Margin of Error. It's not on the Level of Understanding, but on the level of Non Understanding. At that Level we discover where Physics gets its roots," Frank indicated.

"Oh, so you mean reaching the point which you don't know?" Sherilyn asks.

"Let's be specific. Physics is one particular behavioral study. It explores the observation, navigation, and manipulation of particles. That's a pretty good working definition," Frank says. Then he takes a deep breath and continues.

"Quantum Physics is simply an extension of Physics, which studies even smaller subsets of particles and waves. Candidly, you can extend it out to particles and waves so small you actually enter the realm of nonexistence. The mirror principle until the nth degree is involved.

Now you understand the basics of Physics. However complex, we can get inside a sphere of particles and they can be mapped." Frank explained.

"The people intelligent enough to map such things developed the realm of study called Physics. It simply doesn't matter how small or how many of the particles exist. They can be charted and patterns gradually emerge. Some physicists use these patterns to justify the existence of God and Spirit. Others use them to justify atheism. They can be calculated in an infinite manner, so there is no presence of a Higher Power. They see it as merely stuff with a predictable pattern and an understandable rule of margin," St. Stephan concluded.

"Joseph, You can come along too; climb in here with Sherilyn and I. Angie is watching us. Frank is watching, however he's frowning because he knows we're about to discover something big," St. Stephan relayed.

"See how complex the sphere of particles is if you cast an ultraviolet light on it through radium? Then you see it even more clearly. The patterns do something fascinating once you've taken them all. They're infinitely changing," St. Stephan articulated.

"Let's go back in the elevator," the Therapist commands. "Push the button to #1, please."

They leave Joseph there at Level 28 as he watches and uncovers more. After saying their goodbyes to Joseph they return to the elevator. Sherilyn follows the Therapist's instructions and the elevator opens to her office.

"I'm back Sherilyn replies groggily as she wakes up on her Therapist's couch and says, "Did I say anything interesting

Place 33, Secrets of Universal Truths Revealed

Goodbye, Louise

YOU ARE A CHILD OF THE UNIVERSE NO LESS
THAN THE TREES AND THE STARS.
YOU HAVE THE RIGHT TO BE HERE.

Place 33, Secrets of Universal Truths Revealed

Chapter 12 – Ego Discord

We're back in Vegas - A couple days later. Sherilyn had a date with Sterling. They had a little argument at the end of dinner. He asked her how many sex partners she's had over the years. She thought it's none of your business. Maybe the information would be safe with him, she figured, so she told him the truth. He acted okay with it on the surface. But, Sterling hid it very well, at first.

Sterling brusquely told Sherilyn the Elevator of Enlightenment was repaired. They got the keys and drove from the restaurant to the wind tunnel (a.k.a. Vegas Indoor Skydiving) when they stepped inside the elevator.

Sherilyn asked Sterling, "Where exactly are we going?"

He replied, "It's a cousin of The Place; in fact it's next to The Place. This evening we can't go to the Place. There's too much friction right now. This place is called Red Arc."

"What does it look like?" Sherilyn asked.

"There's bright, bright orange and yellow with white clear light all around. The sky is empty here," he says, with his mouth in a tight line. "We're here right now because we're in conflict. I'm angry and irritated at you, because you didn't tell me you had so many sex partners."

"That's it? That's what you're upset about? What about you? You're the biggest flirt I know. How many sex partners have you had?" Sherilyn shouts at him.

Then turning to St. Stephan she says, "I have a more important question. What happens when a man and a woman come together and have intercourse? What happens in the spiritual world?"

"They become one. They are then a whole organism," St. Stephan replies through Sterling who is crossing his arms now. "They are always tied to each other."

"So, if you have a lot of sex partners, you're forever tied to these people?" Sherilyn asked

"Yes!" Sterling shouted.

"That's why you're mad. You believe you are tied to these souls indefinitely. What? I don't understand." Sherilyn questioned his intent. "Is it like a cord attaching each other spiritually?"

"Yeah, in a way," St. Stephan interjects, "The number of sexual partners contributes to the fabric of the individual. You just have more texture Sherilyn."

Sherilyn says to St. Stephan, "Sterling's had a lot of sex partners during his lifetime a lot more than me. Does that mean he has a lot of texture?" (Knowing of course he is his vessel on Earth, he's not going to say something bad about himself.)

St. Stephan replies, "Sterling had sex with many different people in a void. It gave him a certain detachment. Once in a while there are people like this."

"So, can I do this?" she asked, feeling cheated because she didn't know.

St. Stephan replied, "Yes, by gaining the wisdom of clarity, which comes through forgiveness."

"What happens when people have sex with partners of the same sex? What happens spiritually?" Sherilyn asked St. Stephan.

"It magnifies their energy. We're all made of energy. As souls of humanity we have bodies, and the body stores both masculine and feminine energy. Some males are born with more female energy. Some females are born with more male energy. It depends on how the matter configures itself. All should know they are all Children of the 'One Triune God.' They should know they are all loved equally," St. Stephan informs.

"Sherilyn, in the life you're living, you're female," St. Stephan continues. "However, you have a significant amount of masculine energy. This male energy is incorporated into your mindset and the parameters of your soul at present. On balance you're predominantly female, including your mind."

"So it's odd you have an enormous blind spot understanding male-ness. I find it peculiar. You have it, because you don't want to remember. You want to forget many things because you're afraid.

Place 33, Secrets of Universal Truths Revealed

You have difficulty understanding men so you don't collaborate and cooperate with them as well as you could. You're going through a process of remembering, awakening." St. Stephan instructs her.

"Why did Sterling and I get so mad at each other like that?" Sherilyn asks. (Sherilyn is watching a diagram of explanation appear.)

St. Stephan responds, "Ego discord...when you get angry there's a formation of accelerated male energy escaping, being projected, and then gravitating back toward female energy from you. It forms sort of a disk. An appendage is always forming. A third body out of two interacting entities is created. Its Karmic, cellular, molecular, and its atomic in essence you are pure energy. But it's so flat I can only see the edge. It's only an appendage when looked at peripherally. If you look at it from top-down it's a disk. It goes all the way out, around and back into you."

"What does this disc thing have to do with me and Sterling getting into an argument?" She asks.

"Your male wave or vibration got long and it stung him, repeatedly. You have a considerable amount of male energy for a female embodiment. Obviously there's no right or wrong," St. Stephan retorts and continues.

"It's just how you're structured. Your shortwave is the color red, flat, and straight. It doesn't extend too far from you. When you get angry your wave lengthens, because you're adding male energy to your female wave. It elongates; in fact it curves.

The female energy acts as a receptacle or a receiver. Something is triggered and the two become masculine because male energy is dominant. There's a convergence of unmanageable energy.

You could say it's like a small explosion, or at least a spark. There's definitely friction in an energetic context. It's too much charge, so it must go somewhere. This will no longer be with the change in female polarity."

(See illustration ego protection page 150)

"Sterling and I don't like each other right now," Sherilyn pouts.

"Again the issue is male energy. On balance he has more male-based energy as a polarity. You have more female-based energy. The appendage is formed as a departure from your ego discord," St. Stephan continues.

Joseph steps in to impart his knowledge. "The imbalance of energy is revealing. The newly formed appendages are shot out because the male energy in this instance can't contain itself. It's over-saturation for him. When you have an overabundance of energy it must go somewhere, so it leaves the embodiment. The intensity of the friction depends on how far it goes out."

"In your case Sherilyn, it always returns because you're the female pole. Interestingly, no matter how hard you try, you can feel the stillness, but you can't exactly be the stillness. It's a polarity unto itself. You can always find peace. **If you think it, it will be true,**" Joseph replied, hopefully.

Joseph follows with, "I figured out managing male energy means more atoms are involved. It's extra dense and has more aggressive tendencies. Female energy has a gentler, more receptive, passive orientation to its energy. Of course one can't exist without the other. Neither can exist in harmony 100 percent of the time. Something that isn't constant can't always be perfectly sustained."

He continues, **"No matter what the conflict, any discord should be viewed in the language of energy.**

Visualization can help a great deal. Because of the language barrier, most people aren't highly articulate with energy as a language or form of communication. They can't take their feelings, their mental images, everything that makes up the symbols of how their senses are communicating and convert that unspoken stuff into words. It's difficult to achieve with true precision. Obviously, some are pure symbols, which make visualization more accurate. This is why it's instrumental to teach those who don't visualize well.

The problem is, when dealing with patterns of energy influenced by something as extremely subjective and ego-

Place 33, Secrets of Universal Truths Revealed

based as emotion, you can maneuver another individual by bypassing the ego-conscious mind. *Allow them to feel balanced energetically.* However, if they're extremely imbalanced then it's a temporary solution, like anything chronic tends to be.

Start laying a foundation of balance. Children are a good example as to why concreteness is so important. Everything's a metaphor for everything else. When you lay a concrete foundation psychologically in an individual and manage it, balance happens. By being stable yourself, stability in your relationship is the result." Joseph explains.

"Sterling was born expanded," St. Stephan explains. "His unconscious cognitive memory was active early in his childhood. This happens to individuals in present incarnations. These are multilayered, of course. Take their *tapes; lay them on top of each other and they'll all be joined together.
(*Tape: the lifetimes recorded from your spirit)

Start laying a foundation of balance. Children are a good example as to why concreteness is so important. Everything's a metaphor for everything else. When you lay a concrete foundation psychologically in an individual and manage it, balance happens. By being stable yourself, stability in your relationship is the result." Joseph explains.

"Sterling was born expanded," St. Stephan explains. "His unconscious cognitive memory was active early in his childhood. This happens to individuals in present incarnations. These are multilayered, of course. Take their tapes; lay them on top of each other and they'll all be joined together. They can be accessed consciously and they're always being influenced unconsciously or energetically too.

Certain people learn more quickly than others. You can say this is an attribute of inheritance, genetics or coming from a supportive, nurturing environment with highly intelligent and creative minds, guiding and instructing a child as he or she grows. If this individual didn't have layered tapes, from previous experiences, surprisingly it doesn't matter."

"I found when Sterling speaks of tapes, he is speaking about the tape each of us has recorded of our life experiences

Ego Protection

Place 33, Secrets of Universal Truths Revealed

Two people must compromise with each other's egos to build trust and look in the mirror.

They can be accessed consciously and they're always being influenced unconsciously or energetically too.

Certain people learn more quickly than others. You can say this is an attribute of inheritance, genetics or coming from a supportive, nurturing environment with highly intelligent and creative minds, guiding and instructing a child as he or she grows. If this individual didn't have layered tapes, from previous experiences, surprisingly it doesn't matter."

"I found when Sterling speaks of tapes, he is speaking about the tape each of us has recorded of our life experiences on each lifetime. That is why hypnosis works so well. I can access your unconscious tape and rewind and fast forward to get information," Sherilyn revealed.

Joseph is emphatic about understanding energy, and how to manipulate it is an extremely useful tool. "You can coax it, even stroke it. Energy can actually be pushed around," He says.

"How?" Sherilyn asks, "through my words, through visualization exercises?"

"No, actually it happens through projection," Joseph responds. "Clearly it isn't one of the five senses. Energy can feel like stillness, although literally speaking it's never still. Focus, center yourself and feel the stillness of energy," Joseph interjects. If you can project that stillness, you're actually projecting energy. When it interacts with other energy, something else is formed. That's a flexible description of how to manipulate energy; however try it sometime and you may be happily bowled over by what happens as a result."

St. Stephan steps in, "I'll share an example: Projection of energy is the reason why you can stand behind a complete stranger, stare at the back of their head, really concentrate and eventually they'll turn around. Of course you must get yourself still enough, focus hard enough and push the thought toward them. It's simply a manipulation of what is."

Changing subjects from sexual matters, forgiving Sterling, Sherilyn asks St. Stephan, "How can I better understand and implement energy to reflect the material world in a monetary medium?"

"By doing exactly what you don't want to do," St. Stephan responds. "It's necessary to do all the things you feel repelled by when you think about doing them. Examples include being pragmatic, having self-discipline, being focused and clear with good organization, being methodical, and being linear and concrete. This will begin to balance the scale within you.

Given the level you're on, you'll benefit greatly from the disciplines you haven't wanted to undertake. You grasp abstract concepts easily. However, your imagination isn't what it should be. Skin problems are part of your Karmic lesson, but this can be processed out.

You're also paying a Karmic sexual debt, because you shouldn't have sex only for self-gratification, and you shouldn't go against the grain of what you've learned. You'll pay in Karma for that, too." St. Stephan concludes.

"I like to think in units," Joseph reveals. "Your ego unit is about one-third yellow, one-third green, and one-third brown.

Sterling's ego-units start out red, go to pink, and then to blue. What happens is our ego-units form a molecular structure. It looks like a chain. There are six segments following each other around, each one trying to dominate the other.

When observing the occurrence of it, I look at the east side, to the left as you view it. The body of the energy it forms between two organic energy units, male and female, interacts. It's made up of intense emotion." Joseph concludes.

"Balance is the key," St. Stephan states.

"Do we need our ego?" Sherilyn asks. "If we're expanding spiritually, where does all this fit in? How do you get to the best version of yourself?"

"Everything has its place; it's all about keeping things in balance.

The ego needs and wants control," Joseph explains. "Ego energy is unyielding, rigid and inflexible. The core essence of our

Place 33, Secrets of Universal Truths Revealed

Humanity isn't reality-based. When out of balance, the ego-self contains a great deal of fear. The more the ego gets imbalanced, the louder its voice becomes. Conversely, the spiritual voice becomes quieter and harder to hear. When you bring the ego into balance you awaken in the truth. Two people must compromise with each other's egos to build trust and look in the mirror."

St. Stephan steps in, with fatherly love and explains, "This is how you look at your ego. First you must know, you have the gift of your life. Second, you have the gift of creating. Third, focus on one blessing every day."

"All right, Sterling drew a picture of some ego's. We have a picture of Frank's ego, and we have a picture of Sterling's ego," Joseph explains.

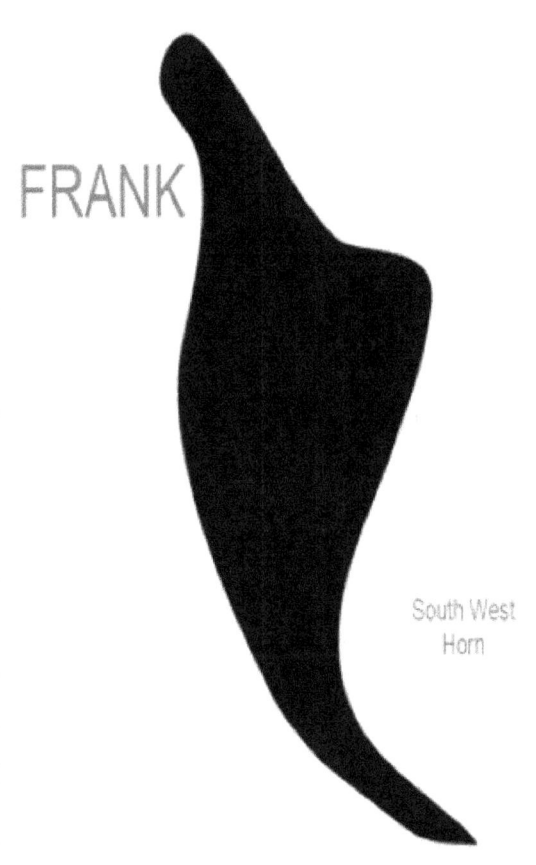

"Why is Frank's ego so pointed? Why is Sterling's ego so big?" Sherilyn asks.

"Frank's ego seems pointed to Sterling because part of it is a reflection of Sterling's perception regarding Frank. It's all-subjective. Sterling sees it that way, therefore it is. Perception is reality," Joseph reveals.

"Okay, right," Sherilyn, agrees.

"Just like anyone's ego...most people understand, seeing things and situations vary. Subjectivity is normal. There will always be a slight variance in beings, yet it is all the same whole thing. This needs to be understood so people accept it. Unless they absolutely refuse to acknowledge this important truth, you shouldn't be afraid to talk to people about enlightened matters," he instructs Sherilyn.

"Okay," Sherilyn ponders.

"Frank's ego is such because he teaches with pain," says Sterling. "He believes pain makes exceedingly clear points and sends a strong message. Therefore, his ego is pointed. Frank's ego also takes on an abstract characterization of what he looks like, according to My feelings and perceptions. But it would be fairly close to your ego right now, if you did the same test Sherilyn."

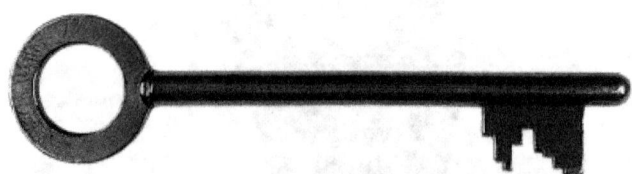

"Really? How do you do it? How can I feel my ego abstractly in order to see it?" Sherilyn asked.

"First, place yourself in the center of your mind geographically. Become as still as you can, and then you free associate," he said.

"You mean don't think any thoughts?" She asked.

"Empty your mind. If you can't do that, think only one thought.

Place 33, Secrets of Universal Truths Revealed

If you can't do that, be as calm as you can. Imagine something very calming," he replied. "Okay, like imagining the ocean?" she questioned.

"Yes. The ocean is good because it's an archetypal symbol. When people picture the sights and sounds of the ocean they usually think calm thoughts. It's out of the collective unconscious mind," Joseph responded.

St. Stephan goes on, "Sterling's ego, as you see it, speaks to the malleability of Sterling's thoughts with peaks and valleys. There are three rounded peaks because he's a slightly feminine, softer, more abstract, muted character at his core.

Looking at him you see an ego, which isn't just unique, but also complex and quite different. His ego has soared through a lot of new thought. Compare it to other egos and it looks new and contemporary,"

"Yes, I like how you made Angie's ego. It also looks contemporary and beautiful," Sherilyn remarks.

"Angie has an aesthetic quality to her that's exemplified through her ego as well. She represents the paragon of beauty," Sterling says.

"Yes, and Joseph you have an ego that looks a little complicated, but it is a nice ego," Sherilyn replies.

St. Stephan continues, "If you have any appendages, they're particularly interesting to look at, because where appendages are placed structurally, it speaks to their particular challenges."

"Oh really?" Sherilyn reacts, noticing she has an appendage.

"Yes, Margot, your daughter has a pointed quality to her ego, for example," St. Stephan explains. "Margot wants to be a good person but can't figure out how. She grows frustrated. She has awareness and an understanding. Being well intentioned will take her farther. She's dragging her past to the point where she's becoming confused."

"This was when she was 9 years old." Sherilyn retorts. "Does color impact our egos?"

"Oh yeah, it represents a person's character," Joseph answers.

"Mine is violet, what does that mean?" Sherilyn asked.

"It means you have the potential to be magical. Not just warm or curious, but healing. It's an outgrowth and the flip side of your own ill health," Joseph explains.

"The violet aura represents health and magic in healing. The pink aura is warm, tender, sensitive, nurturing, passive and attracting. But, pink is not as attracting as red. Red is more sensual. Violet speaks more to the intellect," St. Stephan interjects.

"You have it primarily because of what you've experienced, including your Karmic debt. You'll never escape

Place 33, Secrets of Universal Truths Revealed

it in this lifetime. It's your cross to bear," Joseph informs Sherilyn.

"Really? There's no way out? I don't believe that!" says Sherilyn.

"What don't you believe about it?" St. Stephan asks.

"I believe there's a solution for everything. You can go beyond Karmic debt," Sherilyn states firmly.

"There's no way to avoid the pain of the misplaced actions you've put into motion. You must accept the structure of yourself. You'll gain a special brand of knowledge, which will evolve into your unique style of dealing with life within the margins. You might grow an appendage, which is part of why your symbol is how it is," Joseph explains patiently.

"Why is my symbol like that? It appears I have an appendage," Sherilyn remarks.

"Yes, It speaks to your potential to grow out of it; oh, it's kind of balanced like my ego but a different shape. It's your way out and the path you should take." Joseph mentions.

"The shape of this symbol represents your life. It also represents a composite of what you know and how you deal with life. The appendage is the avenue which gives you hope for a better life. It's grown out of what you know and what you're going through. Due to the misplacement in this life, that appendage is almost premeditated. It was given to you deliberately," Joseph relays.

"How can that be?" she asks.

"Because what makes up the superior God-like quality of Angie has allowed her the luxury of doing this for certain fragments. She wanted to give you an out, however. This will occur at the end of your life," St. Stephan explains.

"Thank you. Angie. What about the pincher part of the ego? We both have that?" Sherilyn asks. "The pincher is the ability of the ego to grasp or comprehend. Those without a strong pincher appendage to their ego lack the ability to grasp, comprehend, or understand easily. The more distinct the pincher is, the easier it is for the ego to seize new information," St. Stephan Continues.

"Can people inherit this? Do they grow or develop the pincher? Do you get it through many lifetimes? Sherilyn asked. Her interest piqued.

"Yes, it's developed through evolving," St. Stephan replies.

"Evolution, I see. My daughter Sally has a tiny ego. She'll grow and her ego will grow too, right? Then she might get a pincher," Sherilyn says.

"Yes, that's correct," he affirmed.

Sherilyn remarks, "Her color may change, too, right?"

"Certainly that's possible; sometimes not, though. Usually our ego color is formed early on. This is because it speaks to the nature of the ego," St. Stephan explains.

"Margot's ego color is yellow. What does that mean?" Sherilyn queried.

"It means she's fresh, receptive, wise and yet unformed. She has a potential for wisdom and for wealth," he says.

"What if you have black in your ego color? What does that mean?" Sherilyn comments, "Frank has that color."

St. Stephan replied, "The ego color black speaks to his sorrow, pain, and futility. He has a suffering quality of life. It also connects to the abyss, the density, harshness, discipline, narrow-mindedness, and the opposite of all things that are white and light."

"...And green?" Sherilyn asked, fascinated.

"Green connects to what you'd expect. Green is the life's blood; it is the potential for the proliferation of life, birth, nurturing, and all beauty in life that's presently alive. Green could be the ego color of a person who appears to be self-serving, but they are truly nurturing themselves to the point of saturation. Afterward they can be more nurturing to other people," he says.

"What about a lopsided ego? An ego that's off balance," Sherilyn wonders.

"A lopsided ego is a person trying to be stable, which is an unstable thought. The intellect is in conflict with the emotions," St. Stephan replied.

"Okay, what does the term 'thuergic' or 'thuergic powers' refer to?" Sherilyn sneaks in one more question.

Place 33, Secrets of Universal Truths Revealed

"Thuergic powers refers to powers beyond the veil in a sour way. It's a bitter, almost insidious desire for the ego, but deeper. It's not a pure thing. The definition is the operation or effect of a supernatural or divine agency in human affairs," St. Stephan explained.

"Sterling's anger, feels like it has dissipated, I feel, its best when you talk things out. No matter how difficult you think the subject is in your ego.

I feel the need to call upon Angie, even though she has been there the whole time listening. Then she appears in a shimmering robe. I turn into my spiritual self." Sherilyn remarked.

Angie transmits, "I am the breath of all before you. With me your life will be filled with light. Follow it. Beware of the P (poison). Follow the A (Angie) and S (St. Stephan); don't be tempted! With me you will be pure and come home."

"Am I on the right path?" Sherilyn asks.

Angie relays, "I'll turn the book over and St. Stephan will look from back to front. (This of course means from front to back on Earth.) To be selfless means to serve one's self. This is a surprising notion for many people. Sterling knows how to read the book." "Hold up the mirror to any lie, hold it up, please. Look in the book of crystal insight. It's crystal clear and incredibly light.

It comes from beneath the tree. This is where I go to write. I love writing about you and all the others. But you're my daughter, 'the misplaced suffering spirit,'" Angie transmits. "I live within Sterling; I'm in his heart. I also live within Sally. I sent her to you; she's the spark willing to convert you to the light and she's St. Stephan's granddaughter, even though he doesn't want to admit his age.

She's full of the energy I impart. You have a partner and all you must do is listen. *The external world is an illusion. On the other hand I am not an illusion,"* Angie relays.

"An Illusion? Why am I not making money? Why am I not experiencing abundance and prosperity?" Sherilyn asked.

Angie relays, "Because you haven't given enough yet. Don't forget the mirror. Always follow the S and the A. You're tempted, and you can convert. Don't be afraid, Sherilyn. Things aren't what they appear. Love will prevail and you'll live in the light. Don't be fooled," she says.

"Why do I have to live out this life of misplacement, Angie?" Sherilyn asks, disappointed.

"Because it's a process of paring out taint and impurity. It's also to gain wisdom, selflessness, and dwell in the light. Once you're with me, you'll teach others. But, you're tempted. Frank lives close by and has a female counterpart under your skin. She smells; she works away and she's tainted. Frangelica, his counterpart, is trying to speak to you. That's her; she's brown, tall and smells like nutmeg. Then she rots you, so ignore her." Angie says.

"I am different. I exist for those ready to bathe in the light. Sterling is becoming a beacon of truth. He's almost there; he's 90 percent full. Frank has no chance now," Angie says referring to Sterling attaining power someday from Frank.

"I'm concerned, Angie. Sterling and I don't get along," Sherilyn reveals. "I am attracted to him, but he's too controlling."

"Don't be ridiculous," Angie says. "It's an illusion. Don't believe it and it'll disappear. He waits on your gifts, so you'll be rewarded."

"Do you see my daughter Margot?" Sherilyn questioned.

Angie replies, "Margot is lead, density. Very dense, I can taste it. She tastes like density, and, her confusion is deep. Her resentment is deeper, and hate is actually love for her. We need to part the wall for Margot. There's a lead wall in between the light and semi-light. You forgot to hold up your mirror, the one in the closet. Get it out and look at yourself. Know who you are and what you're doing." I hand the hymns to you, St. Stephan.

"They're singing hymns within your soul, it's unbelievable, and you don't even know it," St. Stephen relayed.

"You've forgotten your mirror and now they make fun of you. They think you're a fool. They're so confident they're singing. Yes, the longer they remain, the more songs they sing,

Place 33, Secrets of Universal Truths Revealed

for you and, the more difficult your life may become because you don't convert," Angie relays.

"Convert to what?" Sherilyn asks.

"Convert away from the negative, self-serving, self-destructive energy, all the things that make you personal. Convert to the impersonal, selfless, loving, surrendering light that you can be. Only you know why you've resisted this," Angie responds.

Sherilyn knew she was not only talking about her. She was transmitting thoughts about all of humanity.

They started singing hymns again:

> "Heartless may they be-e-ee, Insensitive are we-ee, Male–o– Materially."

"He has a hand in it too," Angie responds. "St. Stephan is the male force within your material world. Be true to your spirit and you'll want not. Heartless, insensitive, material, self-serving illusions are what you're buying, and therefore that's what you'll have to sell. A fool's paradise is nothing more than a stepping-stone in reverse. Why? Because you think it feels good? Why? Because you think you'll have more? Actually you have less. Why? Do you know? Sterling knows because he's considerably older. He knows." St. Stephan says, "He only has ten percent more to go. You're younger, Sherilyn, but you have an opportunity to learn from me, your Spiritual Father, in unison with Angie. To betray this would be tragic. You cannot un-know what you already know. You sought, and you found. But you don't like everything you found. Why? I'll tell you why, because you haven't released your ego yet? A well-managed ego is a marvelous servant. An ill-managed ego makes you a slave. Live between the spaces and walk the line.

You will know. We love you, Sherilyn. Trust in the light my spiritual daughter."

"I do trust in the Light," Sherilyn says, a bit defensively.

"I love you no matter what happens. I love you so much," Sterling says. "I love your creamy body. This is who you really are. This is you in your purest form. You have blue eyes and the creamiest skin. Even your tongue is the same velvety color. You couldn't be more pure. Let's put our feet in the water."

"Okay," Sherilyn smiles up at him.

"I love touching you," he murmurs.

Angie comments, "I have seen a glimpse of the conversion you can help him make. You give him your pure strength. You convert the one-third tainted by light and add to the ten percent confidence he doesn't have yet. In doing so, he draws upon his potential and implements the things we have to share with him." "The presidents have an affinity for Sterling," St. Stephan remarks, "The past United States presidents have a noteworthy attraction to his mind. Andrew Jackson says let's sit down and have some tea. Abraham Lincoln has his hand on Sterling's shoulder. Much earthly sense is linked with Abraham. He was an extremely well intentioned man, or entity still influencing things to a limited degree today.

These entities and their essence are still influential for those who are receptive and open. Call them spirits or ghosts if you like. They're quite real, and I don't mean relatively speaking either. Accept and embrace them. Know they're part of you all. Those who are closer to them are more expanded and older. They all add to the quality of your experience."

"Sterling is a perfectionist with all things that matter. Your daughter Sally and he share a soul directly from Angie. It has a ticklish molecular quality like a sandwich with you in the middle. Like baloney," Joseph interjects.

"Ha-ha, very funny." Sherilyn laughs half-heartedly. "She's like the mayonnaise that spreads easily. He's like the bread, forever fresh. Eat the whole thing and stop worrying. Instead trust in spirit. Pebbles that trip you up distract you easily.

They trip and drip of lessons already learned.

They're insidious little things. They feel familiar, but always have the same result. Spiritual backsliding is useless. Instead move ahead. The more you walk forward, the larger your horizon will become. You must trust or nothing works. I don't like the word 'Faith' too much; I prefer the word 'Trust.'

Your daughter Margot needs you to dream for her. The two of you are defensively reactionary or backward looking. You're like course grain rubbing itself repeatedly and creating friction

Place 33, Secrets of Universal Truths Revealed

and heat resulting in conflict and redundancy. It's almost as if the two of you are pears from the same tree.

Both are trying to escape each other, both wishing there was no pit. But, there is; the pit is the taint. The taint is the misplacement caused by Frank and his cohorts," says Joseph.

Sherilyn stops, looks over to Angie and she connects with her again.

"Love and light dismisses with the game. The game dissolves on the sidewalk of pain. You must trust what you know is true. Margot needs you. Soak up purity and reject taint. It's okay, just remember to relax," Angie says. "I'll dwell within you. Speak and feel from the light and all will be well. Trust and carry your mirror," she transmits.

"We're forming a blanket of truth over you in the elevator. You probably won't remember tonight. But we'll cover you in the truth and you'll remember in the morning. Sleep well, Sherilyn," Angie telepathically relays.

Place 33, Secrets of Universal Truths Revealed

Chapter 13 – They Hold The Cards

We're still in the elevator when Sherilyn asked Sterling, "What's wrong?"

"We have a choice right now," he says. "A choice to make a sacrifice."

"Sacrifice what?" Sherilyn asked.

"My life," he replies, cryptically.

"To kill yourself?" she questioned.

"Mmm-mmm, no" he says. "To sacrifice my life for others. That's what they say, and I don't want to do that," Sterling bellows.

"We are on Level Seven. Let's get out now," Sherilyn requested.

"Frank will you come?" Sterling implores. "Come on down. Come on, Frank. We need your help. Come on, come on please," Sterling begs and pleads with him. Abruptly his level of upset grows even more.

"Where is Angie?" Sherilyn blurts out. "Tell her I love her."

"She is there, watching. I see her clearly," Sterling says trying to reassure her. "She's up very high and on the left. She's rather distant right now. I'm on Level Seven. It's dark but it's okay."

"Should we go somewhere else?" Sherilyn probes.

"No, this is okay; it's okay," Sterling says, his hands visibly shaking.

"Stop!" Frank urges, I have something to say.

Tears begin to well up in Sterling's eyes and he quickly wipes them away.

"It's all right sweetie, it'll be all right," Sherilyn reassures him calmly.

"Hello," Frank says gruffly, as he appears suddenly.

"Hi Frank, how are you?" Sherilyn says, guardedly.

Sterling begins laughing hysterically. It's a nervous laughter. He notices Angie is becoming more serious and is not smiling now. "She knows we're going to move on and end our relationship. We have a choice. She is donned in purple robes today."

"You still think it's funny don't you Sterling." Frank declares gruffly; Sterling wipes tears from the corner of his eyes.

"What's going on, Sterling? You're on an emotional roller coaster right now. Doing that gyroscope thing again," Sherilyn exclaimed.

"Frank just asked me if I want to die," Sterling proclaims.

"What did you say?" Sherilyn probes.

"Well, um, he's listening intently now. He knows it's time for a choice. There's a ten percent chance I'll die in the next week," Sterling tells her.

"What? Really?" Sherilyn is getting upset. "How can that be?

"A car wreck! " Sterling revealed.

"Oh, God! So it's up to you?" She questioned.

"Angie's disappointed in us. She's disappointed in you too, I see that," Sterling verbalizes.

"Why? Why is she disappointed?" Sherilyn asks, suddenly sobbing. You do not want your Guardian Angels, or Higher Self upset with you."

"Angie's frowning. I've never seen her do that before. Frank is being unusually serious," Sterling says. His voice trembling with fear and his cheeks now streaked with tears.

"It's because we cut off the love between us and decided to go our separate ways. Because you feel I had too many sex partners. What's going to happen to me? To us?" Sherilyn cried.

"You're to the right and down. I'm in the middle, smack dab in the middle," Sterling described distinctly.

"Angie's further away then I want her to be. She's unhappy about this decision. You haven't been making the right choices!" His voice is shaking with emotion.

His voice shaking with emotion.

"What choices? What about? Angie, what haven't I been making the right choices about?   Please tell me!" Sherilyn implores. Angie nods her head. "Please come closer Angie," Sherilyn pleads with her.

"She has an apple in her hand, a red apple. I can see it," Sterling says, calming down a bit.

"I see it too. What does the red apple mean?" Sherilyn asks.

"She's wearing a purple robe," Sterling goes on. "It's not covering the sky as it usually does. She's drawn in, almost shrunken. She's not as outspread across the sky as usual. She and Frank have been talking, I can tell."

"Mmm-hmm, tell me more," Sherilyn cries, drying her cheeks.

"I've never seen Frank so serious," Sterling says.

"He says you could die. Are you ready to go?" Sherilyn queried.

"No, not really," Sterling stutters. "Well, yeah my heart's ready to go. My spiritual heart. Actually, my heart is so stressed it could be both, or one and the same."

"Mmm-hmm, because of the way we think here on this plane in this world. Did Angie tell you what was wrong? What wrong choices I've been making?"

"She looks intense; I don't think you want to make her mad right now," St. Stephan expresses.

"Angie please talk to us." Sherilyn is doing her best to listen to Angie's thoughts. "She thinks we haven't tried hard enough and I agree," Sherilyn tells Sterling, plainly.

"Good God! What more do you want from me? What do you want me to do?" Sterling begs Frank.

"Shut up you stupid Fucker!" Frank shouts.

"Frank, you shouldn't talk like that," bellows St. Stephan.

"You dumb son-of-a-bitch," Frank declares. "You and Sherilyn are pure people. You're not of them you're from here. Be yourselves and you'll be okay. Don't stop now. You're getting afraid, Sterling. It's very unlike you. Your loneliness haunts you, and its confusing your mind. Take a step back and watch your mind work; sort it out; lay the options down like cards."

All of a sudden Frank is holding some cards. Frank lays the cards on the table one by one, muttering, "One card for Sterling, one card for Sherilyn, and one card for her daughters."

"Your daughter's card is split down the middle with a white line. The cards are lying on the white table," Sterling says.

"Frank, are you going to sit down or not?" Sterling asks, clearly agitated. Frank sat down without saying a word. "You always gotta fuckin' make it a little harder, don't you Frank! You think, I'm not gonna pass the test! Don't you Frank, you motherfucker!"

"He loves you, Sterling." Sherilyn nervously interjects.

"It's okay," St. Stephan says turning to me. "We're related; he's my brother.

You're watching this, Sherilyn. I see you clearly in the darkness, wearing white. You have blue eyes, bluish-gray actually."

"I don't see it!" Sherilyn replies.

"I don't know why you can't see it. Angie's a little closer, she looks a little larger now, and she's very disappointed. We better be careful."

"Seems like everyone is related here," Sherilyn says. "They're upset because you flirt so much. Ask Frank why can't you be truthful about your feelings and not judge me?"

Sterling shakes his head no.

Boldly she asks, "Frank, why does Sterling have such a hard time being faithful to one person on a date? I need to know."

"Sterling is an insecure, egocentric person," Frank answers. "He has the ability to charm the pants off just about anybody. But that's all he wants to do. In this past lifetime, his parents scared him away from commitment. The deeply-rooted thoughts from his boyhood resulted in noncommittal behaviors."

"I believe that," she says. "So why won't he make a commitment for us to get this information out there?"

"Sterling can help with your children," Angie answers sweetly.

Sterling explains, "The cards are on the table and you're in white. The space is black and we're in the light. We're in between places. Frank is sitting there patiently. He can be rough, but he is always very tolerant."

"What does Angie say, I have to do?" Sherilyn asks.

"Angie says she's going to help one more time," Sterling replies.

"Thank you Angie, thank you. I know you helped me with my misplacement," Sherilyn says.

There's a momentary pause and then Frank answers: He says, "that's it, Sterling! That's it. Stop taking everything so personally. You can meet the challenge of your past. Sherilyn's been helping you. She's a loving, caring person and loves you very much."

Deep inside she knows Frank's words are true. She does love Sterling.

Place 33, Secrets of Universal Truths Revealed

"I guess I've offended you," Sterling mumbles.

"Yes, you have," Sherilyn pouts.

Sterling says, "I've done so much though. In addition, Angie says you haven't done the right things, either. She's disappointed in me and she's also disappointed in you."

"Yeah, what do I need to do?" Sherilyn asks again.

He replies, "Angie says that you haven't helped me enough. You have to let go first. Let go and let God. Let your love pave a safe road. That's exactly what she said. There it is, a yellow path. I see it's full of light. Just go down it and you'll grow. Forget about your past."

"Oh my God," Sterling says, suddenly startled.

"What? What's wrong? Tell me," Sherilyn cries.

"Jesus Christ, that almost killed me," Sterling says breathing hard.

"Frank picked up the cards off the table. Crap, it's the children's cards. Your daughters! He's holding the card. Margot's on the left, the card is face up. He is holding all three now, just staring at them. It's not like him to pick up the cards," Sterling remarks nervously.

"Why? Are my kids going to be okay?" Sherilyn asks, worriedly. She can feel the worry creeping into her voice as tears spring to her eyes.

"I'm not sure," Sterling says, breathing even harder. "He's studying the cards and freaking me out. Christ! I feel like I'm going to have a heart attack."

"You're alright, Sterling. It's alright, I'm here," Angie telepathically relays trying to reassure him.

With a big sigh he says, "Margot's on the left in black; Sally's on the right of the card in red. There's a white line dividing the two. He picked up the card, Sherilyn! Frank picked up the cards!" Sterling cries out.

"Help us, help us Angie! Make Frank put the card back. Please, make him put it down." Sherilyn pleads sobbing uncontrollably. Hot tears spill over and start streaming down her cheeks. "Angie, please make him put the card back down. Please Frank!"

"He's going to take your children, Sherilyn," Sterling breathes in a deep, dark voice. "You need a favor."

"Oh God! Please, Angie help us, my kids, no, please! They're all I have," Sherilyn exclaimed.

Sterling's breathing begins to slow as he pleads, "Angie? Angie, listen to me, please. Sherilyn can't take it. She can't. She won't make it, I know. Please Frank, put, the, card down. Put it down, put it down now.

I know, Margot is supposed to be with you. I know you're not shitting me. Let's let her decide. That's what they want, Sherilyn. They want Margot to decide?"

"Decide what?" Sherilyn queried.

Sterling replied, "Yep, they feel you influence her too much. You're interfering with her Karma. Don't do it anymore! If Margot wants to be with her dad, you better let her be with her dad, okay?"

"Okay," she replied with tears in her eyes.

"Frank, come on, come on," St. Stephan wheedles him into finally laughing.

"Did he put the card back down?" Sherilyn asked, almost afraid to breathe.

"Mmm hmm, yes," Sterling says with a sigh. "Whew! God, you never have to worry about Sally. But as for Margot, let her make up her mind. Or we'll all pay."

"Thank you Angie, thank you very much," Sherilyn said in gratitude.

Sterling said, "Frank could have taken her. It's almost like you're only given so much room to make the correct choice and then they intervene. That's what their purpose is in our lives. You're connected now. Remember all can be prevented through self-sacrifice. You cannot give too many times, without taking away from yourself."

"Oh my God, I will. Let's go back," she says.

Sherilyn looks at Sterling for a moment. She drops her guard and feels his strength and the security his arms offer her as they get back into their body suits.

Place 33, Secrets of Universal Truths Revealed

With her head nestled against his chest she sits still in his energy, drinking in the energy surrounding him. Sterling gently held her away, his blue eyes studying her face.

He says, "The universe has found you worthy. You've been blessed to be chosen to help, and I've been blessed this evening being a witness to our experiences."

Instantly they're back in the Elevator of Enlightenment, then on to Room #333 again to take Sherilyn home. When arrives she gives her girls each one hundred kisses and tells them she loves them.

 Minutes later the phone rings. It's Kenton. They chat for a while Sherilyn has the phone to her ear, looks befuddled, looks straight ahead, and says, "Kenton wants to go on a real date."

Chapter 14 – Margot Makes A Choice

Sterling arrives at the hotel and, as always, Sherilyn tells him, "Lets go to the wind tunnel."

In a few minutes she's ready. They drive to Vegas Indoor Skydiving. It's only 5 minutes away. They go to the Elevator of Enlightenment, then to Level 33, The Place. They found some crystals outside the door and they are playing with them while sitting on a huge lily pad.

Sterling starts telling Sherilyn about crystals: "Did you know you can create an electrical chemical interaction with crystals. The stones have a certain magnetism that both draws energy in them and puts forth energy, too. The stones can be used to manipulate energy in an organized, focused manner or you can cross the energy flow."

With many damaged pathways (from falling off a bar stool), Sterling has created new furrows in his mind or brain grooves.

He continues, "The electrical chemical interactions also have a magnetism that draws energy to them and puts energy out. Crystals manipulate energy very well. So, if you use crystals on any person it's important to exercise care and do it in an organized, focused manner so it's productive. If you miss that, you can wind up crossing energy flows. Always balance energy with caution.

There are some fundamental symbols we are contributing to the new age. Let us start with crystals. Why are crystals so important now? Think about a crystal as you look upon one for the first time. Let's say you find a crystal in a riverbed, what is your first reaction? Probably that it's attractive, it's clear, and, it's hard. It doesn't look like anything else around itself. In fact it doesn't feel like anything else around itself, either.

Why do you suppose that is? Many say it is time for us, a race of living creatures, to find a tangible symbol representing what we need to change - a symbol that emanates from the core of it all. Something core-like that represents light, it is extremely tenacious, and it has certain fluidity at the same time.

A symbol representing everything we believe to be wrong, in terms of the imbalance that exists now. Crystals seem to provide us with this meaning.

Crystals contain energy. Some have many practical, hands-on uses. Crystals are at work, in every day technologies like watches, computers, radios and more.

However we can do more with the energy in crystals. Why do so many of us claim the New Age as something finally ticking, ticking, and ticking, down to something magnificent in metaphysical terms.

We have attached great metaphysical attributes to crystals. Even though they are a hard material, they also represent everything that is Light," Sterling explains to Sherilyn. "They are like solid light."

Sherilyn replies, "Angie is telling me that you are a conduit due to reasons of which I am well aware. Angie says she is the spiritual wife of St. Stephan, your higher self. You and Angie are always in contact and Angie is my higher self."

"Sterling is St. Stephan's begotten son and he will take you to a new, interesting place today." Angie relayed.

"Okay, he's St. Stephan's Son, I get it, I think. I truly love my spiritual mother and I am so lucky. I am your daughter? ...Which makes you my higher self?" I want to be connected with you again," Sherilyn remarked.

"It's good to have a live and let live attitude," St. Stephan continues. "Nothing is ever a big deal--which means it is a big deal. Follow through with your intentions you know are true. You're here to learn lessons, but you also have free will, which means you have a choice. It's the duality again; but truth and fate are real as well."

"Considering your misplacement, you do a lot of things right. You're learning to become more receptive to the five senses from the other world, the other half. You would've had to come back an entire extra lifetime to fix that. You don't have to do that now," Angie telepathically relayed.

"You are very different," Sterling could have lived a life of solitude, been reflective, written. He would have been very prolific; but he chose to help you Sherilyn," St. Stephan conveyed.

"I appreciate that St. Stephan. Why am I different? Because of my misplacement?" Sherilyn asked.

"You're eccentric; you have an open heart and mind, also a quizzical nature. You are a good person, a very, very, good person--more than you know, I think," St. Stephan declares.

"Really? Thanks," Sherilyn interjects.

"That's not enough now to enjoy the luxury of Level 33 and be involved in each other's perfect states. Sterling loves you here, period. He loves you everywhere. But here it's special because he's so pleased to see what you can become. It's about maximizing your potential. This is who you genuinely are at your best, and you look different. We all look different," Joseph, says perched on his log.

"Oh hi Joseph. I know, I'm creamy," Sherilyn sighs. "Can we go to another Level now?"

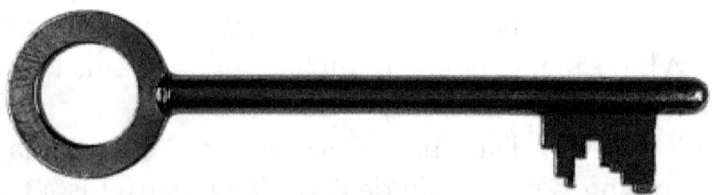

"Angie is smiling and radiating her aura and nurturing rays to you because you asked about her," St. Stephan continues,

"She's shifted her energy on you. Now you're filled with the water as well as soaking up her intent for you, which is about the purest of pure energy. She believes you should pursue your book project.

She's sincerely pleased with you and happy you've come to a higher plane of awareness. This is as it should be. You understand you were misplaced, and, you understand the

Place 33, Secrets of Universal Truths Revealed

whole chronology you experienced. You're moving on with your life in a positive and productive way now, and you'll stay on this track, as long as you go with the flow.

You're in the Light now; don't change it. Be careful because negativity will try to drag you down to its level. People of that ilk, the Unforgiven souls. Angie wants you to be cautious because that's a threat for all of us."

"We forgiven folk who are trying to return home," Joseph stated.

"Associate with open-minded people who thirst for knowledge. And don't worry Sherilyn," Angie sends this thought to Sherilyn.

"Do you want to talk to Frank about Margot?" Angie asks. "Frank is disturbed and grumbling right now. However, he has good intentions for you. He teaches through pain and that's why Sterling suffers as he does. Just ask him."

"Hi Frank, I love you," It's good to show love and respect to the higher aspects of God. Well at least I try," Sherilyn explains.

"He stuck out his tongue at you," St. Stephan says.

Frank is asking, "What do you intend to do with Margot, Sherilyn?"

Sherilyn laughs and she replies, "Gee Frank, my intentions are to let her do whatever she wants. I just want to know if I should do it now, or should I wait until she grows a little older?"

"Frank wants to know if money should play a part in your decision. He knows you're tempted." Sterling says, communicating for Frank.

"I am tempted, but I don't feel its right," Sherilyn exclaims.

"This is your test," St. Stephan says. "Well, it's one of your tests regarding Margot. Through Sterling, you did what you needed to do.

You did what was necessary to even out the situation. Now it's freed up. You're finally in a position to actually choose of your own volition."

"Of course I want to do what is best for Margot. But I'm worried about Sally not being with Margot, because Margot may choose to go back to her Dad," Sherilyn contemplating her decision.

"Frank wants to know, do you think it's healthy for Sally to mimic unforgiving thoughts from Margot?" St. Stephan relayed.

"Of course not. However, she learns from other children, like at school, too. It's such a hard decision. I want her to go with her father for summer vacation to try it out," Sherilyn said, thinking Margot would go for a while and then come back.

Frank says, "If you make the wrong decision, you and those connected to the situation will suffer karmic debt. In other words, you have some control over what happens to Margot."

"So if Margot goes back with him, then she'll pay her karmic debt to him? Is this true?" Sherilyn reiterated.

"Yeah, but she will also pay her own debt, as opposed to riding on the shirttails of Forgiven people, trying to skate, which she's inclined to do. She doesn't want to work, and she's in her position because you were misplaced. All this wouldn't have happened, but it did and you've received a lot of help. All you have to do is make the right decisions. Of course, the right decisions are often the hardest ones to make," Sterling says.

"Sacrificing again?" Sherilyn replied.

"You can't gain anything without giving something away. That's how it works; it's an opposing pair of opposites," Joseph states.

"That's right," Frank relayed. "Generally speaking, the most painful processes are the most enlightening ones. It's hard to do the right thing as people say."

"I'll talk with Margot about it," Sherilyn says. "Okay Frank? Thank you."

The conversation stops there because she honestly didn't know what to do. Margot's father is the man who said he would chop her mother into little pieces and feed her to the dog.

Sherilyn prays, "Oh God. What should I do? I don't want to let my daughter go back to this Unforgiven man. What kind of mother would do this? I must let my daughter, at eight years old make her own decision.

It's unthinkable. Of course they told me in another session, she really is not eight years old. She is an old soul here to learn lessons, like me. But I did not forget Frank's words."

The next morning Sherilyn asked Margot what she wanted to do. Margot tells her, "I love you, Mommy, but I want to be with my Dad." Sally comes running in crying.

Sherilyn calls Sterling. She's crying while saying, "Sterling, Margot wants to go with her Dad. I don't know if I can do it? I can't lose my child. But, I can't let Frank take her away permanently from me. I don't know what to do."

Sterling offers his opinion, "Margot is a frustrated soul. She wants to break out! We all went through this, one way or another. Because she finds herself surrounded by Forgiven people all the time, she is being challenged," he assured her.

"Well, I don't know, if I can send her back there." Sherilyn responds.

"Frank says, 'Yes!' But you know how he teaches. He likes to short circuit things," Sterling responds back.

"I'd rather have her learn with a little pain, than to have her leave me completely," Sherilyn says with conviction.

"She will only go to Phoenix to deal with the conflict. She has no choice really," Sterling replies. "The best way to handle Margot is to teach her respect and do everything that will result in her being calm and stable. She needs roots."

"The roots can be mental not geographic can't they?" Sherilyn probed.

"Then she can get closer and closer to the light. She can make a lot of progress this lifetime. She has to make the decision whether or not to get saturated with the negativity or whether or not she wants to do the harder thing and follow the light," Sterling said.

"Why is that?" Sherilyn questioned.

"Well, it's harder for her to follow the light, right now. She has to make the decision. There is no right or wrong about it. Its just progress," Sterling answered.

This happened after Sherilyn retained an attorney and got custody of her. Sherilyn was so sad even thinking about Margot going back to be with her Dad.

Sally and Sherilyn cried all day.

The following week Margot went to live with her Dad. Sherilyn learned that there are Forgiven and the Unforgiven Souls. We always have a choice. We have a choice to be negative and get saturated with negativity until we finally flip over to the Light and become a Forgiven Soul. On the other hand, we can choose to just follow the Light and be a Forgiven Soul at any time.

Place 33, Secrets of Universal Truths Revealed

Light beings
In the community of the pathways of Neither Time

Chapter 15 – Community of Neithertime

We find Sterling and Sherilyn sitting on the lily pad at the Place.

"I am waiting to leave my body in the Place because I like escaping my emotional pain. I cry ever since my daughter left," says Sherilyn.

Sterling looks at Sherilyn and says, "Let's go up north."

"I'm with you, let's go north toward the blue light," she agrees, nodding her head. Our spiritual bodies are still sitting on the Lily pad."

"Can you see that?" Sterling asked, "What do you see?"

"I don't really see anything. Just blue water and white. What do you see?" she asked, knowing they each have a different perspective.

"It looks like ice, arctic and freezing. I'm looking out at ice and a frozen lake," Sterling responded.

"Can you breathe in this state?" Sherilyn questioned.

Not really; you don't need to," St. Stephan replied. "It's frozen here. I like it even though it doesn't feel cold. The lake is frozen because we are in the northern sector, of the northern hemisphere. I enjoy looking at its frozen blue-white beauty."

"When you leave your body from the Place it's the true departure; we left our spiritual bodies. It feels like we have a residual of a body. It feels that way in my mind Sterling explained. It is all-relative. It is kind of odd and ethereal. Even though it's frozen, the water is so clear. Let's penetrate the ice. Come with me Sherilyn," Sterling requested.

"You go, okay! I will watch from here," Sherilyn says reluctantly. "I changed my mind, I'm coming!"

St. Stephan starts to describe this part of the Place: "It is wonderful in here. I see frozen fish, fossils, and glaciers. I see water coming out from under the ice we just went through. But it is not really ice; it only looks like thick ice. It does not feel hot or cold. The molecular structure opens again and now it is like water, like being underneath the ice."

Place 33, Secrets of Universal Truths Revealed

"I am in awe of the incredible beauty here. It is full of light and passageways," Sherilyn proclaimed.

"There are souls in here as well. The souls are moving around, thinking. There is a couple over there. They do not make much of it. They see us and smile from within a crystal clear tunnel.

They are talking about what they will do next. They are talking about getting a particular block of ice, returning it to where they live and dissecting it." Sterling explains.

"Do they need help?" Sherilyn asks Sterling.

"Evidently there's a whole damn city down here," St. Stephan says, surprised.

"Is that right? Have you ever been here?" Sherilyn probed.

"No, I've never explored this region before. At least I don't remember being here," he replied.

"Let's go down and ask if they want some help," Sherilyn offers.

"What is your name?" Sterling asks one of them.

The soul, who is holding hands with his wife, hears him and tells Sterling his name is Jack.

Sterling then adds, "He wants to know who is talking to him."

"Tell him your name," Sherilyn instructs.

Sterling says, "We are not in our human body forms as we would be on Earth, but they are accustomed to this, so they know we are there as a presence. They are in bodies in this dimension."

"What is he wearing?" Sherilyn tests.

"'Jack' is wearing a long tailcoat," Sterling responds. "Now that I see him and some of the other souls more closely, they almost look as if they are fossilized. They look old, yet fresh and young at the same time. They are certainly different. They look porous with no gills, yet it appears they're breathing through the water. They extract oxygen from the water through their skin. I see a slight ripple in the water. It is an undulating part of the Place, down even deeper. "

"What kind of souls are they? What is this dimension?" Sherilyn asks Sterling.

"It's in the 33rd dimension," Sterling says. "They're serious but happy as they perform their tasks. They are crystalline and pure of heart, they look fossilized," he says, mirroring my observation.

Then Sterling said, "Let's go into the city; come on through the ice."

Looking around Sherilyn sees a soul who appears to be swimming but without much movement. There are tunnels everywhere.

This area of the Place is confusing, like an underwater maze. Some tunnels are glass-like; some are closer to ceramic or concrete in appearance. There are alien souls, they are fossilized looking, it is difficult to describe. Their skin is not soft. Sherilyn reaches out to touch one, a little girl soul sitting with her parents.

The little girl soul says, "Oh mommy I feel something." Sherilyn knows she felt her touch. But how? Sherilyn and Sterling are from another dimension.

"This is Ms. Sherilyn," Jack says to her, introducing Sherilyn to the little girl. "Stroke her hair to make her feel comfortable. She'll feel it in a light, almost imperceptible way," he tells Sherilyn. In the water her hair is gooey and sticky.

"Do they know God?" Sherilyn asked Sterling.

"They are very focused," Sterling declared.

"What kind of tasks do they do daily? Can you see?" Sherilyn questioned.

Sterling replied, "They're putting together Aquarian thoughts for the Age of Aquarius. They're planning to send them for review back to the upper level of the Place.

They intend to be of service to the management so to speak. They will use the information they gather to facilitate Unforgiven souls to becoming Forgiven souls in a place that looks like water, under the thick ice-like structures."

"What's this Place called?" Sherilyn probed. "It has a name doesn't it?"

"Looks like we're approaching the center of the community," Sterling says. "Someone is writing um, okay, he's writing on the wall, '**The Pathways of Neither Time.**' That's

Place 33, Secrets of Universal Truths Revealed

what it says 'The Community of Neither Time.' It's a very clear place. I like it here. The Souls are friendly; it has an excellent vibration, though different. I think they volunteered to perform their tasks."

"Can we have information on how to make the Unforgiven souls Forgiven? Can we get that information?"

Sherilyn is full of questions.

"I don't know yet. They're doing peculiar things with substances I don't recognize. I see a Place that looks like a laboratory where they're working on a project," Sterling answered. "They're floating around almost as if there's no gravity--not floating like we are, but advancing without actually walking, just floating. It's not like a human being or a spirit, more like how a scuba diver propels forward. The whole Place has a sense of floating. It's very unusual."

"What are the colors like to you?" Sherilyn asked.

"Oh beautiful, a lot of gold and shades of blue coming through the crystal clear white water. You see all the colors when looking up, rather than what we describe as our sky on earth. There's a great deal of the white, thick stuff that appears like ice. It seems like they've been here a long time. Wait, there's a female over there named Lydia," Sterling mentions.

"Lydia? How do you know her name is Lydia?" Sherilyn questioned.

Sterling responds, "I don't know. Yet somehow I can tell that's her name. She is reading what looks like a book, but when she opens it there are no pages."

Sherilyn asks, "How can she do that? (*Sounds like an ultra Ipad, but this was 20 years before the Ipad was invented*) Lydia is using a process of osmosis I am not familiar with. She just opens the book and absorbs the words and thoughts. It is about lending time to what looks like a book."

"Interesting? Do they have symbols like letters and words?" Sherilyn asked.

"Well, the answer is yes, but I don't see anything there," Sterling relayed.

"What about their eyes, what do their eyes look like? Do they have black eyes like aliens?" Sherilyn queried.

"Mmm-hmmm. They have black almond shaped eyes, and grayish, creamy skin that's fossilized. Their hair isn't really hair it's a sticky substance, almost oozing from their body. In fact, it starts at their head and goes a little more than halfway down their backs. It's a grayish, creamy color like their skin. They have triangular faces. They do look alien; I just realized these are the white beings that do the experiments. Yep, this is the community down here. It's very old, and they've been doing it a long time. They are Aquarian," says Sterling.

"This is the Age of Aquarius right? Are they from Lemuria?" Sherilyn asked intrigued.

"Yeah, Lemuria and Atlantis are words we've attached to it, but they're busy working," Sterling replied.

"Sweet. Let's talk to Lydia," Sherilyn suggests.

"Sure, okay but we aren't, um, well at least presently, we aren't of this place, not exactly anyway. We're floating out of our bodies. From here we're a long distance away," he trails off.

Sherilyn says, "Hi Lydia, do you mind if I ask you a question? What are you doing?"

She replied, "Well, I'm working."

Then Sherilyn says, "Do you mind my asking what you're working on?"

"No," she says kindly.

"What is it?" Sherilyn probed.

"I'm working on a fractionalized way to facilitate the few positive thoughts an Unforgiven Soul has, to become comfortable with the negative energy that makes up that soul," she replied so matter-of-factly.

"Are you having any progress with it?" ("This is what I need for Margot," Sherilyn thinks to herself.)

"Yeah things are coming along well," Lydia reflects telepathically.

She will put her small project together with the others, then there will be a full composite, and a profile published and put forth for review.

"How long have you been working on it?" Sterling asks.

"It's been about 80-something years now," Lydia responded.

Place 33, Secrets of Universal Truths Revealed

Sherilyn ponders, "I wonder if she's been to the Earth. I'm not certain but my intuition tells me she has been there. She knows I am there but in a different way."

"Are you ready to return now?" St. Stephan asks Sherilyn.

"Yes, I guess,". Sherilyn replied.

"Thank you Lydia," they both say at the same time.

She is smiling at them. They need to go now. They can and will come back here again. They are returned to their bodies on the Lily pad and then to the elevator of light. Sterling says, "Push level 29."

They chat while in the elevator. "I'm not feeling good about Margot leaving to live with her Dad," Sherilyn expresses.

"I know," Sterling tells her. "Its like you embark on a trip. You go through many experiences; you learn from each one all the way there, and all the way back. It's like a boomerang," St. Stephan relayed. "Margot is on a precipice this lifetime. She can become a forgiven person if she meets the challenge. So far she is an unforgiving soul."

Now when she is with Sally and Sherilyn, She's torn in more ways than one. Because Sherilyn was misplaced, Margot is very frustrated. She needs to be with her father who is of the Unforgiven mindset," St. Stephan reveals.

"Well, she has Karma to work off too," he retorts.

St. Stephan said something profound Sherilyn did not hear completely. She says, "Repeat that again. What did you say? People of the light are what, reversed?"

Sterling takes a deep breath. "Mmm-hmmm. People of negative, truly evil thought are not reversed. They are down there, not just down because they must be down. They're really in a negative hell place."

"A-a-ha-a!" Sherilyn says. "I feel like my understanding is clicking into place."

"People of the Light shift to a negative place when they must deal with negative people. But, it's only due to the mechanics of polarization," St. Stephan says.

"I understand. What do you see here on Level 29?" she continues.

Sterling explains, "Others like this place, too. It's not clear; it's close, but it still has… I don't want to use the word tainted. How 'bout it has some tangy energy?"

"Okay, do you see any one? Can we talk to somebody?" Sherilyn asks.

St. Stephan starts explaining what this Place is like.

"People are having fun. They think they're having a blast," he laughs.

"Can we go talk to someone? Let's do it," Sherilyn says, being impatient.

"Oh, I think I have to completely reveal myself to them. That might utterly freak 'em out. I've never done that in a personal way," St. Stephan says.

"Let's try it, if we can," Sherilyn tried to convince him.

He relays, "They think where they're at is completely normal. They're having typical, average conversations--just what you would expect them to be talking about, like what a beautiful day it is. But it really means how orange this place is now. To them it's like the conversations you would have on Earth. For example, on Earth we would mention how beautiful the day is because the sky is blue.

In this place everything's orange. These people live their entire life, in their mind, in this place."

"Really? Where are they from?" she asks.

"They are souls--souls without bodies, but it's just as real to them as what you experience is absolutely real to you. It is a happy place," Sterling says, laughing again.

"Oh, you and I back on earth are in a much worse state, believe me."

"You honestly think so?" Sherilyn retorts.

Place 33, Secrets of Universal Truths Revealed

"No doubt about it, he says. "Where we're from can be a horribly grotesque place. So much pain and suffering. It is too weighted down with too many molecules stuck together. It can be an agonizingly painful place to get around in."

"Okay, let's try to talk to them," Sherilyn says.

"Oh, we're not supposed to do that," St. Stephan replies. "We're just looking. They can't actually see us you know."

"What? Because we're in a different dimension, they can't see us?" she remarked.

"Yes, if we talk to them, I think they would figure they're hearing things--something Frank would do for sure," Sterling says.

"Oh, he would? Sherilyn is laughing because she's getting to know who Frank is.

"I'm sure Frank gets bored and plays with people all the time whenever he's in the mood to do so," Sterling says chuckling.

"There's a couple over by the sea," Sherilyn notices.

"The sea here is fascinating because it looks and smells like oranges. It's stunningly beautiful here. I notice a lot of red-headed people too," Sterling comments.

"Oh, can we go someplace and talk with someone?" Sherilyn pleads.

"Yes, of course," replies Sterling. "We can go talk to the two we know we can always talk to, Angie and Frank. We know they'll always talk back."

"Mmm hmm, yeah, do you want to talk with them?" asks Sherilyn.

"If you want to, sure," says Sterling.

"Are there any other masters and guides we can talk to?" Sherilyn asked.

"I'm close to these two. Yeah there are others. But, I'm close to these souls," replies Sterling.

"Well, let's talk to them." Sherilyn gives in.

"Wait I want to get closer to this couple. They have orange bodies with red hair. How strange. In fact, everything has an orange hue here," says Sterling.

"What's their molecular structure like?" Sherilyn asks.

"On the molecular level it's light. This is a good place," Sterling reassures Sherilyn.

"Of course it's reversed because we're in The Place you know. But the Place for me is *The Place of Clarity*...you know, with the white water. Place 33--this is *The Place of Purity*. Let's go down four more Levels to get there," he declares.

St. Stephan says, "Wait a minute I want to look at these people. Let's see if I can tell what they're saying. Let's walk over there. I'll just tap him on the shoulder once he says." St. Stephan is laughing aloud; "Look at him, oh boy," he says between peals of laughter. "Look at him. This is what you wanted, right? Oh boy, they're freaking out now. Look at him turn around."

"His wife is scared. Look at his child; she's starting to cry. Look! Oh that's not very nice," Sherilyn says wincing.

"Look at him, look at him. They don't know what to do," St. Stephan is cracking up nonstop now.

"You're acting like Frank now, so uncool," Sherilyn remarks. "We better not say anything, it's cruel. They'll get confused."

"Right! Says St. Stephan. "He felt the tap on the shoulder. I know how to move here. He felt it all right. To me it feels like heat. To him it feels like a tap."

"You are so funny. Are all the dimensions like that?" Sherilyn giggles.

"We'll leave them alone. Yes, you can move energy in them all. Okay. Let's go talk to Angie and Frank," St. Stephan coaxes.

"Okay. Back into the elevator for us." Sherilyn takes one more look around and says, "Oh, this beach is so nice. What color would you say it is? Orange sherbet?"

"It has white sand with orange hues and is so cool," St. Stephan described.

"It smells like orange blossoms. It's lovely here. The people here are fortunate to live in this Place."

"And they have babies here?" she asked.

"Yes, they do. They have offspring; they have children," he says. "It is also the exchange of larger thoughts creating

Place 33, Secrets of Universal Truths Revealed

smaller thoughts. It's really larger feelings, making smaller feelings, continuously reproducing. Life is incredibly multidimensional! Yeah, it's an infinite thing."

"Mmm hmm," Sherilyn agrees. "That's why it is so much fun to travel around and take a look at it all. Yeah, you have been doing that for a long time, haven't you St. Stephan?"

"You have too. Mmm hmm, we all started together," he replied.

"Yeah, but some are old souls; some are not," Sherilyn reminds him.

"I'm older than you are!" St. Stephan boasts.

"Yeah, why is that?" Sherilyn prods.

"Well, that is just the way the matter configured itself," he replied.

"Is it because you went out into the world to learn things before I did?" Sherilyn questions.

It's been said that old souls look at life from a "bird's eye view." This could not be truer. When dealing with everyday scenarios, you take in to consideration "the grand scheme of things." This has helped you let go of things that don't matter in life and hold on to the things that do.

"No, it was just happenstance. That's all it was in the beginning. This is why I'm older," he explains. "You don't have to cross a void here because we're in the light."

"Yeah, it's nice. Let's go to Place 33," Sherilyn exclaims.

St. Stephan answers, "This is a healthy place. But 'Place 33' is where we all want to be."

"I know how about, let's go to another Place," Sherilyn just loves traveling all the dimensions.

"Let's go back in the elevator," St. Stephan commands impatiently. "Push the button, please."

Sherilyn pushed the button, and when the door opens the looking out at a purplish, black opening. They walk through the door to another elevator. It's The Unforgiven Elevator. Sherilyn remembers it from the Karmic Tar Place. "It stinks!"

She relays, while holding her nose. "I can smell it before I even walk up to the clanging door."

They step into the damp, stinking, rotting elevator. St. Stephan requests again, "Push the button back up to Level One."

She follows St. Stephan's instructions and the elevator opens to a black, iridescent Place. It has a ghostly, spooky feeling.

"What is this place?" Sherilyn questioned.
"It looks like a place of doom, but it's not," St. Stephan replies.

"It looks frightening and creepy," Sherilyn exclaims. "What is it?"

"It's just a hollow place. Let me go in and look first before checking it out. Come with me, okay?" replies St. Stephan.

Sherilyn replies, "Okay, but I'm absolutely not staying here by myself. I'm very nervous here."

He instructs Sherilyn, "Open the door." They step inside. "Oh, it's the place of doom and gloom. St. Stephan explains. "It's remarkable; it's so dark. It looks like there's nothing here."

Sherilyn asks, "What do you mean there's nothing's here? Why in hell are we here then?"

St. Stephan enlightens her, "There's a feeling of gloom, definitely. It's a fusion of many peoples' negative thoughts and experiences."

He notices the frightened look on her face and says, "Don't be afraid; it's fine. Every Place is okay."

"Yeah," Sherilyn replies, hesitantly. "I've heard people speak of this place on Earth. The Place of Gloom and Doom."

St. Stephan tries to reassure her, but she's ready to run back to the elevator and get far away from here. Shadows loomed. The place reeked of ancient secrets. Her skin prickled. "I just don't like being here...so much negativity; there's no good reason to hang out here," Sherilyn approximates.

St. Stephan answers, "This place is important because these thoughts from certain experiences are meant to be here. It's appropriate for them to exist here. Yes, I know it seems frightening, but it's really okay. Actually it's necessary. Let's go a little further."

Place 33, Secrets of Universal Truths Revealed

As Sherilyn is biting her fingernails, she whispers, "A little further? Really?"

St. Stephan replies, "Take my hand. We're very white in here. In fact, we're the only white things at this Place. It's quite a significant contrast. Boy, it's a huge Place! It's like being in nothingness. To me it doesn't feel bad because essentially we're not part of it."

Suddenly Sterling gets excited, and yells, "Wait, wait! I'm getting goose bumps."

Sherilyn looks at his arms from atop, and replies, "Oh wow, you do have goose bumps. You could almost call them elephant bumps, they're so big."

As they begin walking down a path she shouts, "Look St. Stephan, I see a lake." They look at each other. Her courage is slowly returning.

St. Stephan says, "Let's keep going a bit further." She nods in agreement. "Wow, look at this lake. It's so iridescent blue-black...rather eerie-looking don't you think?" he queried.

"The sand is pitch black. In fact everything is black here. Standing on it is strange; it's cool to the soles of our feet. We stand out in stark contrast to the purple, blue-black darkness. We might as well be Angels here," St. Stephan interjects.

All of a sudden Joseph shows up on his log. Joseph sounds a little dreamy or foggy as he says, "I haven't been here before."

Irritated now, Sherilyn asks St. Stephan, "Why did you bring me here? If we're way out of place and basically don't belong here, then let's leave. Can we just go, please?"

Joseph says, "I understand, but I haven't seen this Place before. Most would find it sinister, but it's not. Truthfully, it's necessary for balance. See, the rock? Look at the rocks around the lake. The same blue-black colored, jagged rock. It's some kind of mineral I think. Malachite?" he says.

"Malachite is dark green with veins of black," Sherilyn thinks out loud. "Maybe it's Obsidian," Sherilyn says boldly.

"No, it's Hematite," St. Stephan corrects them. "It's not as well-known, it's reflective. Let's go inside the cave," he insists tugging at her hand a bit.

"Oh no, I'm not going in there," she says, backing up a step. She's frightened by the inky, black darkness of the place even though they are white in contrast.

"I'll hold your hand," St. Stephan replies, grasping her hand more firmly. She feels safe with him. He appears almost eight feet tall and looks like an angel.

"Okay" she replied.

"This is an old place; it has an old feel to it, Indian maybe? No, Asian I think," Joseph declares. "We are walking forward cautiously through the black, jagged iridescent rock that reflects the darkness."

"Shhh! Great souls, quiet souls," St. Stephan mutters in a low voice. Instantly he's breathing hard, shallow breaths, as if a red-hot scorching ember landed on him.

"They are touching me," he cries.

"Ooh, I feel them too. I've got chills," Sherilyn remarks.

"They're ancient; they've been here a long time. Oh my God! We've been here before," cries Sterling, "a long, long time ago. God, it's coming back to me now."

"This is an intermediate place. All these souls will move on," Joseph says. "They must get comfortable with their negative thoughts before becoming positive. That's why they're here."

"I'm coming out of the rock now!" Sherilyn screams. "That was exhausting, actually. So much stuck energy. Whooooo! We should go back down on the beach now. Its so gloomy and black here, I can hardly stand it."

"The real activity is happening in the particles and waves of the rock," Joseph relayed.

"I've heard of the powers of protection that spiritualists apply to the stone Hematite. It has expanded into the spiritual realm, where they believe Hematite can transform or absorb negativity or evil," St. Stephan informs.

"Yeah, the sea is so immense. It has its own unique beauty, actually. The iridescent horizon is like a monochromatic kind of composite; it's an oil painting. Everything's bluish-black and the sand is even blacker than the sea," expounds Joseph.

Place 33, Secrets of Universal Truths Revealed

"I'd love to paint it," Sherilyn remarked as she's gazing at this amazing landscape.

"Yeah, it would make intriguing artwork. For those who are there, this place is real. There are so many old, quiet souls there," St. Stephan comments.

"Wow!" That got Sherilyn reflecting on how many souls truly exist in the rock. Is there an infinite number of souls?" she inquired.

"There once was an infinite number. However, over time the souls have merged. There are exceptions though. You see, some souls are so advanced they're incompatible with the emergence or melding of most souls. They stand out! There are a limited number of these souls. This is subject to change although. Currently there are only 28 advanced souls, Supreme souls, those that haven't merged. Or you could say souls within a parameter that stand alone," instructs St. Stephan.

"Only 28 of 'em? How is that?" Sherilyn asks, while getting lost in the story. "You know everything Sterling; you're the Guardian of the Elevator of Enlightenment," she teases. "You reflect the pool of knowledge, right?"

"Well, Some how I know, they're capable of merging with an infinite number of other souls stuck together that make up the masses," Sterling answers. "Well, some souls are so advanced that they are incompatible with the mergence of or melding of most of the souls. They stand out! And there are a finite number of them. But this is subject to change also. Right now there are only 28--that is all, that haven't merged. They are capable of merging with all the other souls that are stuck together that make up the masses."

"The mass thought?" Sherilyn questioned.

"Yes, but there are only 28 finite souls within a parameter that stand alone." In this state Sterling ponders the thought, 28? "That's funny I didn't know that."

"You know everything in this state of consciousness." Sherilyn laughs.

"Joseph continues without acknowledging my little joke: "It's a beautiful place to me. It is not beautiful to those who are

193

here, and it's not truly Hell either. People aren't on fire; it's merely an Amorphic place. I'm using the word in a negative fashion, but these souls aren't forgiven."

"Not Forgiven! Sherilyn shrieked. "That's why I don't like it here."

" Let's go back to the elevator," St. Stephan agreed with her. "They can't hurt us."

Sherilyn said, "Amen to that! Bye Joseph!"
They are back in the elevator almost as quickly as they said it.

Place 33, Secrets of Universal Truths Revealed

Level 29 - Tangy Offspring

By Sherilyn B. Avalon

HOW DO YOU GIVE A LITMUS TEST FOR FORGIVEN AND UNFORGIVEN?

You ask the Soul how much
would it take
To kill someone?

Would you say, "name your price?"
Or
I would not ever
think of doing that! Never!

Place 33, Secrets of Universal Truths Revealed

Chapter 16 – Magnetic Energy

Just to remind everyone, each time we are doing hypnotic voyaging, when I say Sterling we are in the 3rd dimension when I say St. Stephan we are in the other dimensions.

Sherilyn pushes the button for Level 33, and in a blast they are there again.

"Okay, let's step out of the elevator into the water," Sherilyn suggests. "I like to sit here, on the lily pad."

"Do you want to talk to Angie and Frank?" Sterling asked. "Angie is large right now."

"What's she doing?" Sherilyn wondered

"Just looking, yeah, she's very large, and is always to the left, to the northeast part. If you look up in the sky, it's not blue. Really it's not a sky; that's the definition I give it. Everything is clear...white, clear. That's where Angie is, right over there taking up a large area," St. Stephan says pointing to the Northeast sky.

"Mmm hmmm, really?" Sherilyn says.

"Yeah. Oh she takes up about two-thirds of the sky really. Frank is down on the right," he describes to her.

"He isn't big?" Sherilyn shrieks, a little perplexed.

"Oh not like Angie is, no," St. Stephan sighed. "It's because he has more molecules. He would be to the Southwest in The Place as always and down to my right. Balance. It's like this yin-yang sort of thing. It has to be this way. Consider the difference between Margot and Sally. Margot is earthy and Sally is ethereal."

"Oh, I see. Yeah you're right; it's remarkable," Sherilyn remarks and ponders, "I still don't know if I did the right thing by sending Margot back to her Dad. But Margot chose her path," she comments.

"There's no right or wrong about it. It was necessary," he assures her. "Yeah, it's just balanced polarization. It's always that way," St. Stephan illustrates. "When you find someone with like energy, then you magnify yourself. That's what compatible people do. That's what compatible energy does."

"Hmm. I believe Kenton and I are a good match," Sherilyn retorts, watching Sterling's face.

"When you try to synchronize or meld unlike energy, in other words, opposing poles, it's like trying to put the same ends of a magnet together. It doesn't work. You can't do it. It repels.

That is, if you're of light energy, you're the same. In other words you're of the same pole," Sterling enlightened Sherilyn.

"So then you stick together?" Sherilyn questioned.

"Yeah, that's right! It's comfortable, easy, and it feels right. Opposing poles can't attract so you have to be careful about that," he says.

"Mmm hmm, all right," Sherilyn notices, Angie's listening and smiling.

"Tell her I love her, and Frank too," Sherilyn clarifies.

"Angie has a warmhearted smile for you. She says she loves you very much. She can see you, and she knows you're here. Frank says hello, too," Sterling replied.

"That's nice. Tell Frank I said hi," Sherilyn said.

"He says you are doing better now," St. Stephan relayed.

Sherilyn replies, "Yeah, I guess, I am. Can you see Angie?"

"Of course," Sterling says. "She's well. I've never seen anything with such dimension. Anyway she wants to talk to you."

"Oh, okay," Sherilyn comments, her lips turning up into a smile.

"Angie wants me to tell you," St. Stephan begins. "Sherilyn we love you very much and we're sorry you've been misplaced. But, now you're almost back to where you were supposed to be, or at least as close as you'll get in the lifetime you're living now. What Angie has done will work for you now," St. Stephan recaps.

"Thank you, Angie. I appreciate it so much," Sherilyn replied.

"She says 'any time you need her she will always be there'. All you have to do is ask," St. Stephan informs her. "You can just curl up under her gown and she'll bathe you with light."

"All right. Thank you Angie," Sherilyn takes a breath.

Place 33, Secrets of Universal Truths Revealed

"Frank is pleased," St. Stephan continued. "He doesn't feel he has to take any more action now."

"That's good. He scared me," Sherilyn remarked.

"The cards are still on the table. I can see them; everything is the same. That's funny, those cards scare you don't they?" St. Stephan asked. "Frank knows that. So does Angie. The cards are around because we don't control that part. They're in control of the cards."

"Mmm hmm. Okay, ask them what's our next move?" Sherilyn bellowed

"Our next move is up to us," Sterling said. "They primarily watch us, Sherilyn. You can call it judging; but it's more like watching. They're not critical or judgmental until you do something seriously out of line for your lesson. Then they may intervene, but that's relatively uncommon."

"Except with us," Sherilyn snapped.

"Yes," St. Stephan pauses. "Let's put our feet in the water. Soak up the water. Fill the crystal with water and let's fill up through our feet, as we drink the water. We're about one-third full."

"It's fun to feed it to each other through the crystals," St. Stephan teases with a broad smile. "It's a good thing, drinking the pure water of the Place."

"I'm really lucky to know you St. Stephan, and Sterling," Sherilyn boasts. "It's so pure and so refreshing. We need to recharge because life can sometimes get you down. It's such a beautiful place to just sit and feel."

"It's as warm, pure and calm as it gets today," St. Stephan basks in our surroundings. "We bring a different energy to the days here. The place fills up with our energy."

"What do you mean?" Sherilyn questioned.

He replied, "In other words when we're feeling turbulent, it's turbulent here. It stirs up Frank, and it stirs up Angie.

The molecules move faster, like boiling water here."

"Back on Earth do we control the weather?" Sherilyn asked with enthusiasm. "We control our thoughts, right?" she quizzed joyfully.

"There are many interconnected influences, relative not just to the weather but to things in general," St. Stephan justified. "I'm certain that when there's severe weather, the interconnected activity between the forces creating the weather, the people experiencing it, and the living things experiencing it are dancing together. It's all-relative. People can change the force of the weather," he interjects.

"How? Through prayers?" Sherilyn inquired.

"Mmm hmmm. Yes, through prayer, meditation, and through the consolidation of thought. Yes, they could and have changed forces as powerful as the weather. Ordinarily it's not so, but it has happened," he replied.

"Is it up to our brains yet?" She's referring to the water at the place. She wonders how 'filled-up' they are while sitting on the Lilly pad.

"It is up to my right ear," Sterling points to his ear in the material world.

"That is where I felt it too," Sherilyn, replied amazed.

"We're filled up now. Let's go back," Sterling cajoles. "Remember this: if you are worrisome, say you are having guilty thoughts, impure thoughts, then you have negative thoughts in your system. This results in having a sludgy system, a system that is not moving energy well. A system that's not moving the impurities of your body well, you will slow yourself down and then you get a toxic build up.

Even though there may not appear to be a connection…if you have fear, and thoughts of failure, then it's impossible to care for your body. So it's important to purify your thoughts. Do it long enough and you'll purify your body too.

Make sure you know where the genesis of the negative thought is coming from. You need to clarify if it's coming from within, or from without."

"I am having guilty thoughts about my children," Sherilyn confessed. "Once again I had to sacrifice and surrender."

"It's unconscious guilt. If we become too deep with guilt, it's not healthy. You want to keep the roots of your guilty feelings relatively shallow. 'Abel the Enabler' will help you," St. Stephan says?

Place 33, Secrets of Universal Truths Revealed

"Abel has enabled us to do that. How exactly?" She queried.

"By stepping three steps to the right, three steps forward, two steps to the left, and one step down. Then step back and put his hands in front of your face," he replied.

"Or you can ask God to place a boundary around the feeling of guilt, a concrete foundation where the roots can't go anywhere. Abel is dealing within the spirit realm, the realm of the collective," St. Stephan verbalizes.

Sherilyn sits back and visualizes as she watches this spiritual looking character, which looks like the fool in the Rider Waite tarot deck. In a blink of an eye, he's doing these crazy steps on the water in front of her.

Sherilyn Bridget Avalon

Place 33, Secrets of Universal Truths Revealed

Chapter 17 – Alpha Beta

Sterling and Sherilyn look to the left. The door opens. They exit the Elevator of Enlightenment into a place Sherilyn has come to appreciate so much.

"I love Level 33, The Place. It's wonderful here. We see lessons in the sky, alphabet letters and numbers in spheres floating above us." Sherilyn is sing dancing through the doors.

Quickly, Sterling becomes St. Stephan and we see Joseph sitting on his log.

"Who chooses the lessons for people Joseph?" Sherilyn asks.

"It's all about the sphere from where you've originated," Joseph replied. "The question speaks to a larger issue about balance, before understanding anything else. If you're from a certain sphere of energy that's out of balance, the fragments from that sphere must learn a specific lesson to improve its balance. You must look at it in a larger way. A plethora of alphabet soup and each symbol has its own meaning."

"Joseph knows a thing or 2 about soup." Sherilyn snickered.

Joseph continued, "The numbers almost yearn to speak aloud. Eight equals infinity. Ten equals wholeness. The English alphabet has a direct correlation to numbers in code. Each letter is a biological symbol. Each number has a direct opposite and equal numeric pull. Eight also equates to the letter "S." The letter "X" equates to the number two, and, the letter "T" equates to the number "10."

There aren't enough letters in the English alphabet to communicate suitably with words. Only 26 letters are used. There should be 33 letters in the alphabet. Whether added or subtracted the rest are fragments. You can determine the equivalent numbers by applying what you know, as the meaning of numbers and converting that meaning into the new letter.

Seven letters are missing. The reason? There aren't enough letters to stifle growth until saturation is attained. The revelation of the mystery manifests itself. There are too many sounds coming from our mouths. Many sounds aren't represented with the English alphabet considering only 26 are used. With the additional seven letters added all the different intonations correspond with the letters. Instead the opposite has occurred.

Simple words like "you" have too many letters, representing more than one inflection. This isn't communicated in a clear manner. A disproportionate number of letters corresponding to the sounds you communicate with results in excessive ambiguity. Rather than, one letter with many sounds there should be more letters that correspond to singular sounds. That's why there should be 33 letters.

The opposite of the "A sphere," the letter A, is the "V sphere." The bar that is crossing the middle of the letter "A," results in the numerator or denominator of the symbol. Bars in the Alpha Beta, your alphabet, are equivalent to the mathematical division symbol.

A line drawn horizontally is the bar separating the numerator and denominator of that symbol. The "V Sphere" equates to: things starting with 'V:' Vibration, Viper, Venom and Venereal. The "A sphere" associates with words like Angie, Africa, Air, Acceptance, Aries, and Apex. The "E sphere" is the opposite of the "F sphere." The most common bar denominator missing causing an imbalance in the "F sphere." The "E sphere" is balanced with its three bars. The "F sphere" is top-heavy leaning towards Frank's formula.

Energy in the "F sphere" always follows the path of least resistance. A formula Frank uses which is why his energy always follows the path of least resistance. This is why it's so much easier to be destructive than constructive. It's easier to not apply yourself as opposed to applying yourself and coming closer to achieving your highest, ascended potential. It's a formula applicable to all matters of movement between the poles. Frank's primary formula of implementation is this one. The "F sphere" of Failure propels it because it likes excess weight. It attracts negative energy away from the light. It seeks density in all things."

Place 33, Secrets of Universal Truths Revealed

"As far as the Ascension goes it means to transmute Fear and all its derivatives into it's polarized opposite... love and all its derivatives," Joseph conveys. "It is to remain within balanced polarization so that all electrical frequencies and vibrations are within the Love fields. It is to shift consciousness from ignorance into knowing and from separation into oneness.

Within an energy context the "F sphere" is also the opposite of the "E sphere" with the lowest bar missing, resulting in imbalance. The imbalance of Fear is the most important piece.

You might think the code between the letters and numbers could be easily deciphered in a linear way. But there are seven missing letters. Therefore you must re-arrange and move the letters to correspond with 33 numbers, each of which has same meaning. Then you understand the code."

"The knowledge from Alpha Beta is vibrantly alive and working. The Greek biological symbols of energy are represented in the Alpha Beta, your alphabet. It came from the planet Alpha Beta—the third planet in the second galaxy away from Earth. It's a planet that cannot be seen, only felt. Alpha Beta is also a dimensional wavelength at play in telepathy. This energy visited the Greek people thousands of years ago." St. Stephan explained.

"Telepathically, etheric biological 'micro-chips' were embedded in the minds of Greek people, resulting in many advances in civilization including the alphabet. The chips are implanted in the minds of people from places dimensionally different than what we know. You cannot physically locate these chips in the body. They are organic energy and escape detection by the naked eye. It is crude to believe you'll find a substance like a computer chip in the body and reason 'alien forces' implanted it in the people's brains. This isn't how it works.

These 'micro-chips' will never be found because they don't exist in physical form. However, they are actively present in many people. About one third of people have them.

Surprisingly, all but three percent of people the chips lie dormant." Joseph told us.

"Why is that?" Sherilyn asked confused.

"Three percent of the population is all that's necessary to create influence. More people with active chips would be too much. In the future, more chips will be activated as the population can handle the information, these people will constructively convey." St. Stephan informed us.

"Break the code and a new revelation will be your blessing. Numbers are biological symbols in the lines as they are drawn. Look carefully at the vertical and horizontal bars. Attempt to figure out with the letter symbols, the same way as with numeric symbols what the energy is.

With the alphabet the easiest ones are the linear bar symbols such as the letters "E" and "A." Again, "X" equals "2" and "S" equals the number "eight" "W" is a nuisance letter. The letters "W" and "M" fit together in some ways." Joseph relayed.

"They have their ups and downs," Sherilyn says jokingly.

"You want to be an "S," St. Stephan tells Sherilyn. "With an "S" you'll travel far. You're hard to catch, you're sleek, your smooth, and, you're malleable."

"The strongest structure is the letter "A," the first letter in the alphabet. The "J" likes to catch things. They are curious; they have a hook and a stable platform. "T" props up information and provides a crossroad. It speaks to the directions of north, south, east and west, a very stable symbol. That's why the cross Jesus Christ died upon was a symbol of the letter "T."

"The letter "O" refers to infinity as well as the abyss. The letters standing before the O stands on a threshold of things infinite and the abyss. Letters after the "O" stand for challenges met. They have stood on the threshold. They have been through the abyss. They are down the road, continuing, and, they've made it through." Joseph shares passionately.

"Is that linking to a name?" Sherilyn asked.

"A name, words, acronyms whatever it may be," St. Stephan replied.

Place 33, Secrets of Universal Truths Revealed

"Wow! Okay, let's say we're looking at the word "OPEN." Sherilyn puts forth. "Explain to me energy wise exactly what does it mean?"

Joseph Steps in, "Let's look at the letters individually for the answer. We have the "O," the "P," the "E," and the "N."

"Yes, what does it all mean Joseph?" She asks, eyes wide with enthusiasm.

"Symbolically speaking: the "O" stands for infinity and the eternal return of things in general. The "O" also represents the abyss, seen in the bottomless pit at the center of the "O."

"P" is a highly stable and linear north south thing to hang half of the abyss on, and half of infinity on. Therefore, the "P" represents half an understanding.

"E" is powerful because it incorporates the linear post, a balanced post, which is archetypal. It is a kind of magnet it has three prongs. Top prong is positive, the second prong is ground or neutral energy, and, then we have a negative prong. Two "E's" together form a closed circuit or circulatory energy. The "E" is very electrical.

Finally, "N" represents closure, the North-South pole, as well as a diagonal pole connecting North-South pole.

"Odd as it may seem, put it together and you have the meaning of the symbols for the word OPEN."

"That's pretty amazing," Sherilyn exclaimed." I never knew that."

"Put the formula to work using the code and words can be broken up and deciphered," Joseph helped to explain. "The combination creates an understanding of the two opposite sides of the same code. Between the Alpha Beta biological symbols and the numeric symbols combined, it results in a third awareness and a deeper understanding of words and what's truly happening below our level of vision.

This understanding allows you to progress faster so you can be at the cutting edge of awareness. It is a beautiful event, truly beautiful. Alpha Beta energy is the smoothest energy you will find, it is smooth, long, light and transparent. It is entirely instantaneous. Still in time of course, it is Infinite. You now have the ability to understand Alpha Beta energy through code," Joseph says.

"Does eight transform into 33?" Sherilyn asks.

"Very powerful and real, the number "8" it speaks to the infinite principle, the infinite truth. The three's tie in with eight, but only when you put them together face to face, which is why St. Stephan refers to it as a lacing. Like a keyhole unlocking the door between the physical into the spiritual."

"So do you and your signature become more powerful when you sign your name with the number eight?" Sherilyn asked.

"Yes, absolutely," Joseph nods affirmatively. "The '8' is just a symbol. However signing your signature this way is symbolic of what a person knows and where his or her intent lies. Occasionally some people will take note. That person will become pivotal to you. Enlightened people will note how you sign your name. Most people aren't close enough to this unconscious knowledge to recognize why they're so curious. But some actually get it. You will want to gravitate towards those types of people and interact with them. These people are more powerful."

"Thank you Joseph, I appreciate it. We should be getting back. Please tell Angie and Frank I love them," Sherilyn remarks.

"Angie is smiling at you." St. Stephan says.

"Even though I'm grumpy and irritable?" she replied. "She knows you're challenged by your own deficits—the deficit of misplacement, the deficit of an upside down numerator. Look in the mirror and you can right your balance. Remember Sterling is a beacon." St. Stephan advises.

Place 33, Secrets of Universal Truths Revealed

JOSEPH CAMPBELL

"God is a metaphor for a mystery that absolutely transcends all human categories of thought, even the categories of being and nonbeing. Those are categories of thought. I mean it's as simple as that. So it depends on how much you want to think about it, whether it's doing you any good, whether it is putting you in touch with the mystery that's the ground of your own being. If it isn't, well it's a lie. So half the people in the world are religious people who think that their metaphors are facts. Those are what we call theists. The other half is people who know that the metaphors are not facts. And so, they're lies. Those are what we call atheists."

- **Joseph Campbell**

Chapter 18 – Joseph and the Protoplasm

The phone rings and its Kenton. Sherilyn looks at the caller ID and answers." Good evening Kenton," she says in her best seductive, yet casual voice.

"Are you ready to go to the magic show?" he asked.

"Yes we are," Sherilyn answers excitedly.

"Be there in five minutes," he says.

As she helps Sally get ready, Sally tells her she is excited to meet Kenton. Sherilyn introduces them. The two meld energetically as soon as they met.

"Its nice to meet you Kenton," she boasts, in her sweet, most angelic voice.

"Are you ready to see some magic?" he asked, his heart melting.

"Mmm-hmm," she says, and off they go.

That night, Sally was the little star of the show. She went on stage with magician Lance Burton and he levitated her. Then he gave her a magic kit and autographed it. She thought she was the luckiest kid in town.

When we returned to the room, Sally thanked Kenton, gave him a kiss on the cheek, and then thanked him again for the great magic fun.

"So sweet," Kenton murmurs. "But I really like her Mommy."

After several minutes of pleasantries we sit down close together. The sexual energy begins whispering again, this time very loudly. Sherilyn is aware that Kenton wants to take her in his arms right here and now.

In fact, I know if Sally were not there Sherilyn probably would have submitted to his charms with no hesitation. Sherilyn pulled away, fearing Sally would hear.

He runs his finger delicately over her face. She already knew he would be a kind, gentle lover. Probably the best lover she would ever have. Sherilyn eventually caught her voice. "I'm sorry; can we continue this when Sally's not here?"

"Sure sweetie," Kenton says with all his southern charm oozing through. "How about tomorrow night?"

Place 33, Secrets of Universal Truths Revealed

She felt the sexual tension between them. She felt it from the first time they met when their knees touched in his office. The desire for both of them is hot and heavy. "I can hardly wait," Sherilyn whispered.

"Yes," he mutters between kisses, "tomorrow."

Sherilyn walked him to the door. She thanked him for a wonderful evening.

"See you at 8:00 pm," he says, still kissing her. Having a hard time leaving, he finally pulls away with a sigh. "Okay baby, I got to go."

Five minutes after Kenton leaves the phone rings. It's Sterling.

"Can you meet me at the tunnel?" He asks. "Frank is going to talk with Joseph about his Transcendence. You don't want to miss this."

"Are you serious Sterling? What do you see? What's going on?" Sherilyn questions him.

"Meet me at the tunnel. I'll be there in 15 minutes. See you there! The wheeled sphere, the tape it turns," he interjects. " By gotta go!"

He just loves confusing her, although she finds it so intriguing. Sherilyn calls the baby sitter and heads over to the tunnel after she tucks Sally into bed.

She's at the wind tunnel. The doors are locked. Then Sterling. Appears and leads Sherilyn to the elevator of enlightenment. "I'm so excited to see Joseph again," Sherilyn conveys.

They venture out, of course. Both of them are sitting on sort of a pod, watching the blue babies and blue embryos. "They're very nice to look at," Frank interjects, crouching in his usual position.

"Where are they from?" Sherilyn is so curious.

"They're from what you identify as the Atlantean's," Frank answers.

"They're from beneath the water. Frank decided we should view them while he's in a good mood," St. Stephan recites.

"What do they look like?" she queries St. Stephan. "Because of course, when we go to the Place, Sterling turns into you... St. Stephan his higher self now."

He chuckles. "Oh they're beautiful and interesting," St. Stephan continues. "I'm seeing them because Joseph talked about protoplasm when he was alive on Earth.

Frank wanted him to see it's more than what he said. First, he forgot to mention protoplasm has a blue hue.

The blue tone is significant for anyone who interprets things within the perception of polarity. He can't describe something as singularly as he did, um, with his remark on the video regarding reactive protoplasm."

He was referring to a video Joseph Campbell made with author, journalist and commentator, Bill Moyer back in the 80's.

"Let me tap into the pool of knowledge." Then, St. Stephan recites: "Protoplasm: The colorless material comprising the living part of a cell, including the cytoplasm, nucleus and other organelles."

This is a mistake Joseph realizes quickly. Frank is showing Joseph protoplasm. "This is protoplasm Joseph," Frank points out. "Why can't you see protoplasm, has blue energy above the biological reactive substance of its animal nature? It also has a spiritual nature.

Even though it's a rudimentary thing, these two aspects, the spiritual and the animal, work together in conjunction with one another."

"Now Frank instructs Joseph to take a good look," St. Stephan describes.

"In the review of his life Joseph erred by over simplifying, or eliminating, half the polarized condition in the information he released.

In his review, Frank wants to make sure Joseph understands this. As he traveled further down the path of his own life lesson he was about to open the door to transcendence.

He started falling back and falling short, not completing his previous thoughts due to his own subjective ego, fear of death."

"Mmm-hmm," Sherilyn replied.

Place 33, Secrets of Universal Truths Revealed

"This skewed Joseph's perception of things," St. Stephan continues. "Particularly when he grew closer to death. Now Frank wants to make sure. It's like Frank is beating Joseph over the head with it."

"Mmm-hmm," Sherilyn murmurs again.

Fear was something Joseph knew well. Frank asked, "Joseph why were you in fear?"

"Because I failed," Joseph answered.

"That's right, you failed right into my sphere," Frank laughs.

"His, sphere?" Sherilyn queried.

"Frank, Fear, Failed. It's all within the same sphere of energy, the 'F' sphere. Joseph's hook was implanted, you know the hook of the letter 'J.'"

"Mmm-hmm," Sherilyn agreed again.

"That's how it works. Joseph got caught up in that," St. Stephan remarked.

"You knew your challenge," Frank relayed to Joseph. "You recounted it to others giving your own experience. It was to reject lust and fear. Reject the knowledge of it. And you communicated the situation well. However, when challenged with it personally, your own subjectivity, your fear of your own death and of your own ego came up repeatedly. It tainted your thoughts. This made it easy to successfully trap your spirit.

So look at the protoplasm now. You can finally see it for what it really is. Simply explain it to yourself and you'll have no fear. There's no fear here; there's only knowledge." Frank concluded.

"Mmm hmm, so explain it Joseph, please," Sherilyn cajoles.

Joseph talks now. "The embryos are blue because they speak to the spirit. A few can see while in the earth's sphere what would be ultraviolet radiation, mechanically speaking, the electricity of energy bouncing off things."

"Hmm," Sherilyn contemplated his words.

"This is part of the polarization, observing things in their entirety. I wasn't doing that at the time. I was trying to reduce things into a singular thought, ignoring polarity," Joseph said.

"Sterling can see what he sees through the feeling in the silence. He allows his mind to be so open and flat, it touches all sides of his existence. Others can do this too. He's good at sorting out the things he sees. Nothing is ever all one thing. I should have stopped myself when I was speaking to Moyer that day and I should have said, "Excuse me, the truth of it is I'm not quite myself."

"Mmm-hmm," Sherilyn comments, "I know you were speaking from your ego self. Maybe hypnosis would have helped you back then. Did you ever try that Joseph?"

"No, I did meditation," Joseph continued. "Color speaks to the spiritual quality of matter. Most people see virtually in black and white. Those who don't are at the opposite end of the color spectrum.

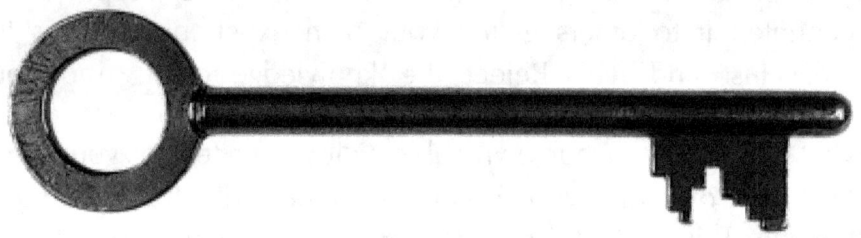

They see colors other people don't see. Violet is particularly important. Blue is of great consequence. I should have been more clear on core issues, like how to position your mind toward any given thought or grouping of thoughts. I'm referring to discussions of how to see both sides of the polarity and to form a triad of the **Wise perspective, knowledgeable perspective, and balanced perspective**

"It's putting your mind between the two poles," Joseph continues, "No matter what you say or think, keep in mind there is a *diametrically opposite experience also occurring* while you're thinking it, saying it, or listening to it."

"Then put your mind in the middle. You want to have that juxtaposition, while speaking to a person or a group. Keep that polarity in mind while thinking or analyzing something. This way the polarization of your mind is balanced. You've become as expanded as can be. Then you'd never say something like what I said." Joseph explained.

"Hmm," Sherilyn is listening to his words intently.

Joseph continues, "Funny because I knew better. But the fear gripped me. And, other things on my mind were distracting me. I was growing bitter, too. I was beginning to feel the loss of what was familiar."

"Mmm-hmm, were you ill? What did you die of?" Sherilyn questioned.

"Ultimately I died of old age," he chuckles. Then he laughs harder. "I died of a rotting body. I knew it was rotting. We might as well call it what it is…"

"You died from cancer?" Sherilyn felt bad.

"Yes I had that too, he says. However, it was a multiple process thing. My immune system was giving out and I was experiencing distress. Mostly I suffered an emotional death, even though I was aware of everything happening. I was about to be reborn into another form. I was shackled to my ego, and it skewed my perception."

"I see, but why's your foot in the cement? What does that mean?" Sherilyn asked.

"It's to teach me a lesson, he replies. I lost my footing. It's like running a race. When do you know you lost the race? At the end, not in the beginning, not in the middle; you know in the end."

"Ah, right," she agrees.

"I lost my race in the end. I could have won. But I chose not to. It was a conscious decision because the race was within my own mind," Joseph explains.

"What about the log? Why are you sitting on a log?" she asks.

"The log represents something I am not to fall off. The log represents stillness, calmness, which equates to my own center, or being centered and still. What do you do when you sit on a log?" Joseph asked.

"Be still," Sherilyn replied.

"Yes, and the more still we are the more expanded we become. Therefore sitting on the log is appropriate; falling off the log is not. Losing your footing is a metaphor for being unable to complete the process of metamorphosis from my ego death. Funny because I talked about it all the time while I was on Earth- the death of my physical self, my natural self, resulting in the birth of what obviously would be my spiritual self. The cycle is complete. The two halves are whole and I betrayed my own wisdom. I gave into fear, which is a common failing," Joseph admitted.

"I'm sure you're not the only one. Yes, a multitude of souls make that mistake. That is what we're about to release--fear. Time for that sphere to move on," Sherilyn says to console him.

"No, but I knew better. The God that the Hebrews constructed for people's minds is a God of domination, of subjugation, a warring God, a God that embodied aggressive, male attributes. It pushed the Goddess aside. It was the death of the Goddess, the nurturer, the sensual, the procreator, and the birth of the destroyer, Zeus. It was the birth of the dominator, the aggressor, and virtually all that overtook the Goddess energy.
Odd as it sounds, I'm referring to The Anti-Christ. This gave rise to the dogma of the Christian religion," Joseph says, looking down.

"That's how polarization works," he continues. "The Catholics attempted to resurrect the balance with the Virgin Mary, 'The Goddess.'

It was misconstrued or actually deliberately manipulated by the extremely male dominant energy of the time."

It almost made it, but even that was misinterpreted. People of intelligence wouldn't believe the notion of a virgin birth. That's not what it meant. It was a ridiculous thought. The birth of Christ was a metaphoric birth, like Buddha being born from the side of his mother. Once again this story was propagated by men."

Place 33, Secrets of Universal Truths Revealed

"Mmm-hmm," Sherilyn repeats, keeping Joseph's stream of conscious thoughts going. It speaks to the human animal, and all that it embodies into the new virgin spiritual self. That's what the virgin birth is about," Joseph relayed.

"Right," Sherilyn agrees again.

"If God, didn't live in all of us and wasn't the other half of himself we wouldn't recognize one another; and if we didn't live in God and weren't the other half of that energy, we wouldn't recognize one another either," he enlightens Sherilyn.

"Really, why is that?" she questioned.

He replies, "You can only recognize what's familiar. That's how you know when something's truly foreign; but even that's a trick. If you recognize something as foreign, then as infinitesimal as it may be, there's something in that thing that you are calling foreign, in terms of reference that is also identifiable within yourself.

"This was meant to be viewed as a metaphor, a spiritual birth. The virgin birth speaks to the polarized opposite — the death of what?

"Hmm, that's interesting," Sherilyn, ponders the thought.

If you can't identify something within yourself at all, when viewing something outside of yourself, you can't see it."

"That's why the notion of God being totally unlike yourself and unattainable, in terms of purity, is an absurd notion. It's unfortunate that most people's fear is so great.

A small number of men have been at this juncture for millennia, about five thousand years. It's so easily injected into the minds of both men and women--thought. There must be balance," he states.

"Sterling coined the appropriate word, 'Femanale' which represents woman and/or man. It's both female and male energy balanced. This is a very good thing," Joseph assured Sherilyn.

"The word 'Femanale' will connote a balanced energy. Balanced energy, bipolar energy, the God and Goddess will face

Sherilyn Bridget Avalon

Place 33, Secrets of Universal Truths Revealed

each other on equal ground of influence, with strength, purity and enlightenment. This will result in peace of mind, an energetic peace. Of course this is a balance Christians don't want. Christ intended equality for men and women because he was both. Both genders and he knew it. He believed in treating others with godliness and the consciousness of Christ. This was attainable for virtually anyone, that is, anyone who worked hard enough, and is willing to surrender their ego to the extent, that they can be balanced for other people and themselves. It speaks to a spiritual balance, and a spiritual respect to the polarity of men, women, nature, spirit and on," Joseph declared.

"Of course it was completely misinterpreted by the warriors of the time. The warring groups started evolving and intermingling with the more Gregorian people, the farmers, the growers, and the nurturers of the land. That's when we start seeing the rise of the male aggressor dominating the nurturer goddess and her fertile energy. It's just the way the pendulum swung. Of course, this is beginning to change," Joseph says with a knowing glance.

"Inventing or reinventing words is powerful," Joseph states.

"Getting the message of what the Femanale is all about out to the world is important. Both genders will be attracted to the 'Femanale' balance slowly at first. The momentum will culminate into a dominant new thought. When I refer to dominance, I mean a dominance to finally achieve balance."

"You see it in symbols, riddles, poetry and metaphors. The symbol of Eve eating the apple when God said don't eat it; is representative of taking responsibility for your own actions," Joseph expounds.

"Right," Sherilyn agrees with him.

"You should be open with your bisexuality," he directs Sherilyn.

"What? No, that was when I was younger," she shakes her head.

"Do you know why you relate so well to men?" Joseph asks Sherilyn.

"Oh, I guess it's because I grew up with only brothers?" She mulls over the thought. "I understand their needs, I guess. I'm not sure why. Maybe it's about male energy matching?" Sherilyn relayed.

"There's a simple answer," Joseph continued. "You as the human animal and human spiritual being--you are both. You encompass both male and female energy. If you were all female energy you couldn't relate to man and vice versa, because of how life has structured itself. It could have gone many other ways, but this is how it went.

The energy dictates you can't recognize Sterling or any other males without being part male or masculine yourself. Sterling can't relate to the female Sherilyn or other women without being part female himself.

This is a fundamental spiritual truth. That truth deserves acceptance, reverence, contemplation, and implementation to help achieve balance. It should be taught in church," Joseph suggested.

"Yeah, I totally agree," Sherilyn, said with a smile..

"It's so fundamental. We're all both male and female energy. If we weren't, we wouldn't recognize each other. That's how it's structured and how it evolved," Joseph relayed.

"So some people have more or less male and female energy than others. And you're saying I have more male energy than most women?" Sherilyn probed.

"Yes absolutely, which is a good thing," he confirmed. "You received that through random fate times karma. It's a good thing, but it would be better if you were more honest about it.

It involves much more than overt sex acts because, as Sterling explained earlier today, it speaks to the crack that keeps yawning open. Eventually it will become a canyon. Whatever's going on at the surface is also the opposite experience going on, of course," he explained.

"In the Spiritual World?" Sherilyn clarified.

"Yes, and if it's a natural interaction such as a sex act, there is a spiritual dichotomy of an experience occurring at the same time. Without that happening at the same time you wouldn't have

Place 33, Secrets of Universal Truths Revealed

sex in the first place. That may be a difficult concept to grasp," Joseph explained.

"Yeah, I don't understand exactly," Sherilyn's voice trails off.

"Well, that's because it involves a perception beyond your five senses," Joseph replied.

"So, in the spiritual world, Kenton and I are having sex?" she asked.

"No, you and Kenton are playing out a *polarized interaction of energy*. It has nothing to do with sex. It's a manifestation of the natural, basic instinct within the five senses of your earthly dimension. Primarily, you're aware of what's taking place on the flip side. It's just as energetic, maybe even more energetic," he explained.

"It's something that could be explained by Eastern religions in your world at this time--in particular Kundalini. In the Western world this is more difficult, because the social life situation is so masculine in its nature. It's exceptional for a person to begin thinking logically about what's going on. For a minute let's change out the word 'think' for 'experience.'

You must experience through a medium that doesn't involve your five senses. Like the experience of 'sex' in this case is going on within your senses. Imagine the opposite of what all that could be: the opposite manifesting experience," Joseph explained.

"Of course," Sherilyn nods.

"Then you'd have at least a fragment of perceptual light on the matter. That will clue you into what's really going on," Joseph added.

"Nothing works without polarization, correct?" Sherilyn confirmed.

"Correct," he nods emphatically.

"The fact that you can't see it is a moot point because it relates to the parameters of the dimension you're in. That speaks to the connection between time and space, and in your case the five senses. This is where imagination can be so rewarding. You can't imagine anything that isn't real anyway," Joseph says, smiling.

"Yeah right, it's real in the spiritual world. I've heard that before," Sherilyn admits.

"Think of the antithesis or the opposite, and you're on the right track. Pretty soon you won't be thinking, you'll just experience. That's as close to a definitive word as possible, given what we're trying to explain," St. Stephan interjects.

"Okay," Sherilyn agrees cautiously.

Joseph relays, "I should've taken this as far as I'm taking it here, relating it to you. On Earth while teaching and writing, I was almost there. I almost made it, I almost won the race, but of course I got stuck."

The style of discourse in this kind of admission is truly a revelation for you. Why? It is because you will end up with a much more progressed world, much more balanced world, and much kinder world. We need to return to this fertility. We need to get back to nurturing on balance, especially now. People like you and Sterling are contributors.

He has the potential to be a principal contributor coinciding with his primary energy. Unfortunately, Frank, grinning with delight right now, has chosen to intervene in Sterling's life in a way that's preventing his highest good to come to fruition."

"I know it is a shame, it is real shame," Sherilyn agrees.

He continues, "Sherilyn, if you'll surrender, the nurturing will be restored. It will allow him to prosper in every endeavor. You'll have done a great thing for your Karma, for the evolution of what'll occur, and you'll please your Mother Angie.

Then you can scurry home at the end of this particular chapter and you can osmose under her skirt along with St. Stephan at her side. Finally, the metaphor will be balanced.

This isn't happening solely by you of course. It's energy at work. Energy's a collective thing. In fact, some energy accelerates at a faster rate, which equates to going further than other energy, even though it's basically the same stuff.

Place 33, Secrets of Universal Truths Revealed

These concepts should be taught in churches and houses of worship. What is energy? What does it mean? What's a metaphor? What does it mean? What does organized religion offer that parallels energy? What does it mean? How can energy be harnessed? How does this result in a more progressive, expanded quality of life? It's all about expansion.

Why is the mirror principle of polarization legitimate? Why is it so difficult for most people to understand? Why is it so unbelievable what you appear to be doing isn't what you're doing at all? It's the opposite of something else. **It's about understanding the makeup of God in Spirit and Nature.** As two halves of a whole, the expanded thought is that of a triad. It's a legitimate concept. Why is this so difficult for people to understand?" Joseph insists.

"Well it just is," Sherilyn snaps defensively, her head spinning with questions. "I'm sorry Joseph. I didn't mean to snap at you."

"If there was balance in bi-polarity this wouldn't be so difficult to understand. You literally are "new" or should I say you're rekindled in a reborn, kind of sense. It will start developing into part of your real world. You won't be dealing with merely your five senses anymore. You'll encounter the spiritual side of yourself along with the senses involving your physical existence. If you can, you'll reduce the pain, take the pressure off yourself, and allow your feelings to radiate forth. Follow your feelings and people will gravitate your way. You sort it out. You neutralize. There's too much intensity here. Between females and males. Neutralize the acid and the friction," Joseph bellowed.

"Okay. However, Joseph I just got out of a bad relationship and I don't like someone telling me what to do. Sterling is a little too bossy--not when he's St. Stephan. When he's one with his higher self, he's perfect. Thank you, Joseph. We must be getting back. Thanks for all your information. We love you," Sherilyn replied; walking to the elevator, back toward her reality.

"Wait, I want to check something out," Sterling blurts out. "Joseph is coming with us. Let's go back to the Elevator."

"Joseph can go with us to the Elevator? Really?" Sherilyn questions.

"Yes, he can come," St. Stephan, answers.

"But isn't his foot stuck in the cement?" Sherilyn replied. "Yes, although as you see, he's missing his foot. He can go in the Elevator by changing his molecular structure," St. Stephan replies.

"Isn't it getting any better?" Sherilyn queries.

"Sure, eventually he'll get it back. But, eventually can be a long time. So go ahead and push the button for Level Seven," St. Stephan instructs Sherilyn.

She pushed the button for Level Seven and instantly they are there.

"This is what Joseph wanted to see. They call this the Hangman's level," Sterling informs Sherilyn.

"I thought it was Mysteries Revealed?" She counters him.

"Well we're about to reveal a mystery. I need a pen and paper please," Sterling asked with his eyes closed.

From the third dimension Sherilyn gives Sterling a pen and paper. Sherilyn explains--when in the seventh level (dimension), that's like a big hand coming down from heaven.

"Joseph wants to explore," St. Stephan relays calmly.

"Seven represents not just the principle, reality and phenomenon of the eternal return but also how we get hung up with this belief," St. Stephan explains; "It's easy to get hung by the number seven. The seven is considered a lucky number because people know innately after every seven there's a new beginning, and also a death. This is why marriage Therapists refer to the seven-year itch."

"There's a pattern in life, and in nature, applicable to the eternal return in many arenas, in respect to the principal and force, and reality behind eternal return. For example, every seven years many things die and begin anew," Joseph states.

"I'll give you an example: every seven years on a biophysical cellular level, you become a new being. You have a new cellular body. If you have a persistent health problem, never give up. If you're patient enough, the body often renews itself.

This is another example why patience and maturity is vital for enlightened people. If you're patient enough, and can endure

Place 33, Secrets of Universal Truths Revealed

the pain, you'll establish a new beginning. In this instance you'll see a new beginning of your cellular body," St. Stephan continues. "This is why Joseph wanted to come today. If you have dead cells at the end of a seven-year cycle, you'll be reborn.

You'll be rejuvenated due to your new cellular structure every seven years.

This also occurs if you have a neurological problem. It doesn't matter which medical problem you're experiencing. If it's a physical problem, the source is your cells.

Reduce stress, boost your immune system, and stay the course. Under an attack of cancer, if you make it to seven years after the cancerous cells are cut loose you will go into remission. It's the same way with something viral. With an illness, if you make it from the inception of the disease for seven years, then you'll be well again." St. Stephen explained.

"That gives us new hope. Maybe we can use *Longevitology?" Sherilyn interjected.

"The reason is because you'll have all new cells in your body. Cellular regeneration is real. New cells are forming every minute; a cell has a life of seven years inside our bodies. The cells of our bodies are constantly dying and reforming," Joseph conveyed.

"Better words than 'dying' is to say our cells are restructuring all the time. A kidney problem can go into remission. If you have no other problem, your body will take the part of your organ left functioning. It will remain functioning from that point forward. After seven years all the old cells are replaced with new cells.

Then, you have another life of seven years. If there is no new disease present, you'll have a healthy organ the rest of your life."

"What about AIDS (Acquired Immune Deficiency Syndrome)?" Sherilyn asked.

"Because of the complex nature of AIDS the body feeds on itself. The trouble with the seven-year cycle with AIDS is the same thing occurs if someone makes it seven years." Joseph continues, "AIDS is a retro virus, which creates a new challenge for the body. It's not just about replacing new cells. Even healthy cells begin to be unaffected by the powerful drugs that normally rid cells of the virus. Gradually it becomes more difficult to find substances that'll penetrate a cell, rid them of viral contamination, and allow the cells to become healthy and whole. That's the difference between a retrovirus and a conventional virus.

Conventional viruses enter our cells. Through the body's natural immune system it will rid the body of the virus. Then the cell is healthy again and the person is healthy again. Retrovirus cells literally feed on themselves.

Drugs can slow the retrovirus down to a point where there are many more new cells and the number of bad cells is reduced. The old, diseased cells are replaced within the seven-year cycle. Gradually only new cells are present."

"There are seven's in pairs, which equate to conscious awareness and the life below. This provides the foundation of water. Many believe it's below your level of awareness, below what are influential bodies of probable thought. A thought isn't a thing yet; it's the possibility of a thing. Here under the water, beneath the unconscious mind, Joseph has hooked into some new information," St. Stephan explained.

"The probability of what is yet to come?" Sherilyn questions. "My daughter Margot once told me, 'Mom, you're like a starter culture. Without you we wouldn't exist. We couldn't rise to our fullest potential.' I thought that was very sweet of her to say. I'm sure Margot is Forgiven now."

"A starter culture is a microbiological culture which performs fermentation," Joseph continues. "Starters usually consist of a cultivation, colonization and fermentation. Yes you can help in the process of cultivating **Femanale Energy.**"

Angie telepathically says, "You are microcosms for what is going on. Frank, the black night, I, the white queen, and you the forlorn and separated daughter. You are a fragment of myself incarnate."

Place 33, Secrets of Universal Truths Revealed

"She wants, and feels the need to attract you Sherilyn," Joseph says. "She wants you to write." She hands you the magic wand of crystal light.

Joseph continues, "Angie says she's a daughter as well. Her mother is dead, and transformed she trans-mutated into her. She says an archetypal force was once her mother and gave birth to her. Her name is Athena. She was born a male but trans-mutated, then had a metamorphosis of energy and became bi-polar and Female in her appearance--still a warrior, but with the ability to conceive & propagate Life. Angie is her daughter and now that she is gone, Angie presides.

Angie is the new energy! ...the new force, the new mass on balance, larger than the polarized Frank. The New Femanale Energy!"

"You are speaking of the Greek Goddess Athena? Ok, I guess you could say I am part of a starter culture in the exchange of energy," Sherilyn interjects, "from Male and Female to Femanale, a more balanced energy."

"Yes, are you ready to get started?" Joseph Asked her.

Sherilyn Bridget Avalon

Dante's Inferno

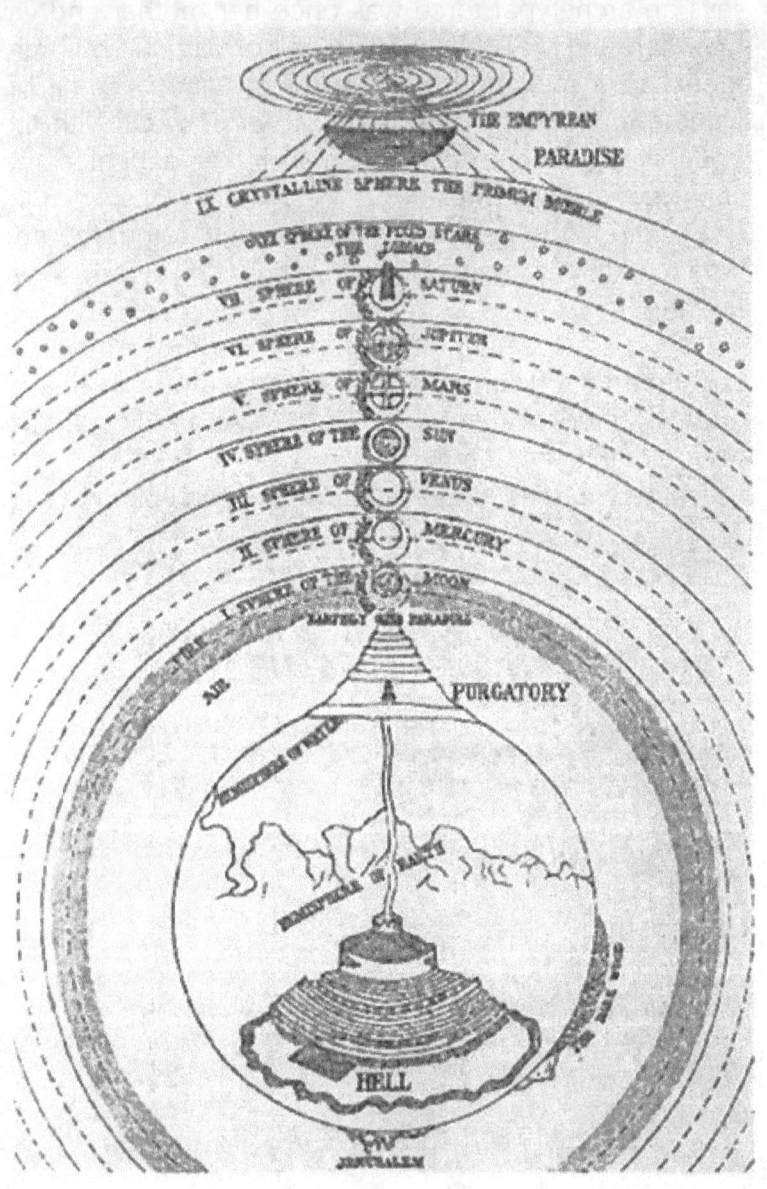

Place 33, Secrets of Universal Truths Revealed

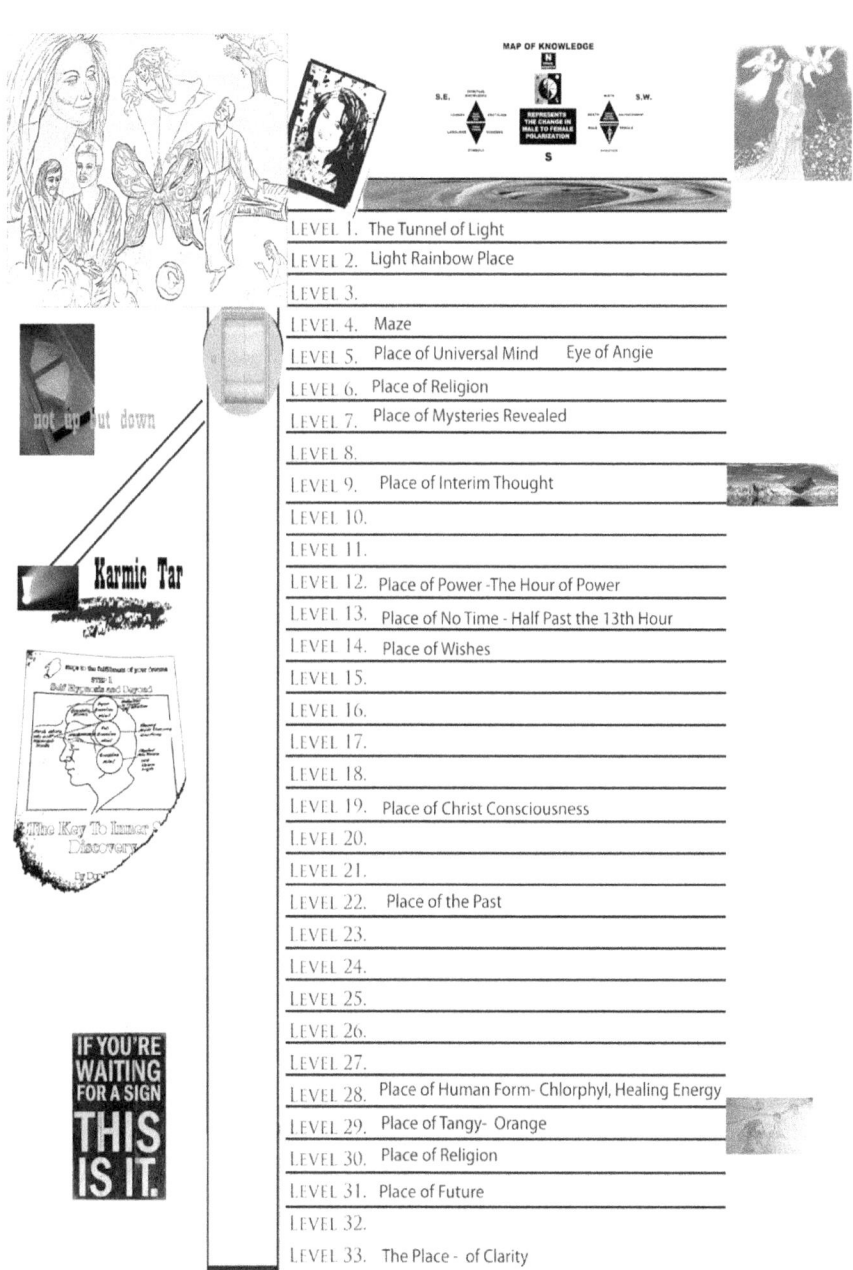

LEVEL 1. The Tunnel of Light
LEVEL 2. Light Rainbow Place
LEVEL 3.
LEVEL 4. Maze
LEVEL 5. Place of Universal Mind   Eye of Angie
LEVEL 6. Place of Religion
LEVEL 7. Place of Mysteries Revealed
LEVEL 8.
LEVEL 9. Place of Interim Thought
LEVEL 10.
LEVEL 11.
LEVEL 12. Place of Power -The Hour of Power
LEVEL 13. Place of No Time - Half Past the 13th Hour
LEVEL 14. Place of Wishes
LEVEL 15.
LEVEL 16.
LEVEL 17.
LEVEL 18.
LEVEL 19. Place of Christ Consciousness
LEVEL 20.
LEVEL 21.
LEVEL 22. Place of the Past
LEVEL 23.
LEVEL 24.
LEVEL 25.
LEVEL 26.
LEVEL 27.
LEVEL 28. Place of Human Form- Chlorphyl, Healing Energy
LEVEL 29. Place of Tangy- Orange
LEVEL 30. Place of Religion
LEVEL 31. Place of Future
LEVEL 32.
LEVEL 33. The Place - of Clarity

To be continued……

Place 33, Secrets of Universal Truths Revealed

References

©NATIONAL ENQUIRE, (JULY 2, 1991)

JOSEPH CAMPBELL FOUNDATION
THE HERO'S JOURNEY

AMITABH BUDDHA- HTTP://BUDDHISM.ABOUT.COM

HEAVEN, BUDDHISM, BAHÁ'Í FAITH, HTTP://WWW.BAHAI.US

GOSWAMI, A. (MAY, 2012 09). CENTER FOR QUANTUM ACTIVIST. RETRIEVED FROM HTTP://AMITGOSWAMI.ORG

MLA: "DR. AMIT GOSWAMI, PH.D. THEORETICAL QUANTUM PHYSICIST." N.P., N.D. WEB. 18 FEB. 2013 <HTTP://AMITGOSWAMI.ORG/>.

MLA: "INDIVIDUAL HUMAN EXPERIENCE WITH DEATH AND THE AFTERLIFE" N.P., N.D. WEB. 18 FEB. 2013
<HTTP://ENCYCLOPEDIA.COM/DOC/1G2-3406300018.HTML>.

Georgian Orthodox) Stephen I of Hungary, known as "St. Stephen of Hungary", in Hungarian "Szent István király" (Catholic) Stephen the Great, King of Moldavia.

*Longevitology- the study of healing Qi energy

Joseph Campbell
I believe Joseph Campbell came through the hypnosis to relay unfinished information. But we make no claims to his establishment or to hurt anyone in any way.

Sherilyn Bridget Avalon

Place 33, Secrets of Universal Truths Revealed

Some info about "The Place"
Looking down on the 33 levels from bottom of the elevator.

HUE WITHIN A HUE, ABSTRACT, ABSTRACT MAZE

Some more info about "The Place"

The universe can be described as "positive existence" (or just simply "existence") Anything outside of the universe (i.e. the met-averse) can be described as "Negative existence" (which is not the same as non-existence).

Negative existence does not mean something doesn't exist; it means it exists beyond space and time in a "reality" that we cannot even begin to comprehend. (til now)

The visible world is the imperfect and changing manifestation in the world of un-changing archetypes that are found in the collective unconscious of humanity.

An Archetype is for example: the form of a ship is abstract and applies to all seagoing vessels; as different as the individual manifestations of ships might be, the form never changes

- Author Unknown

Place 33, Secrets of Universal Truths Revealed

Can you find your mental compass ?

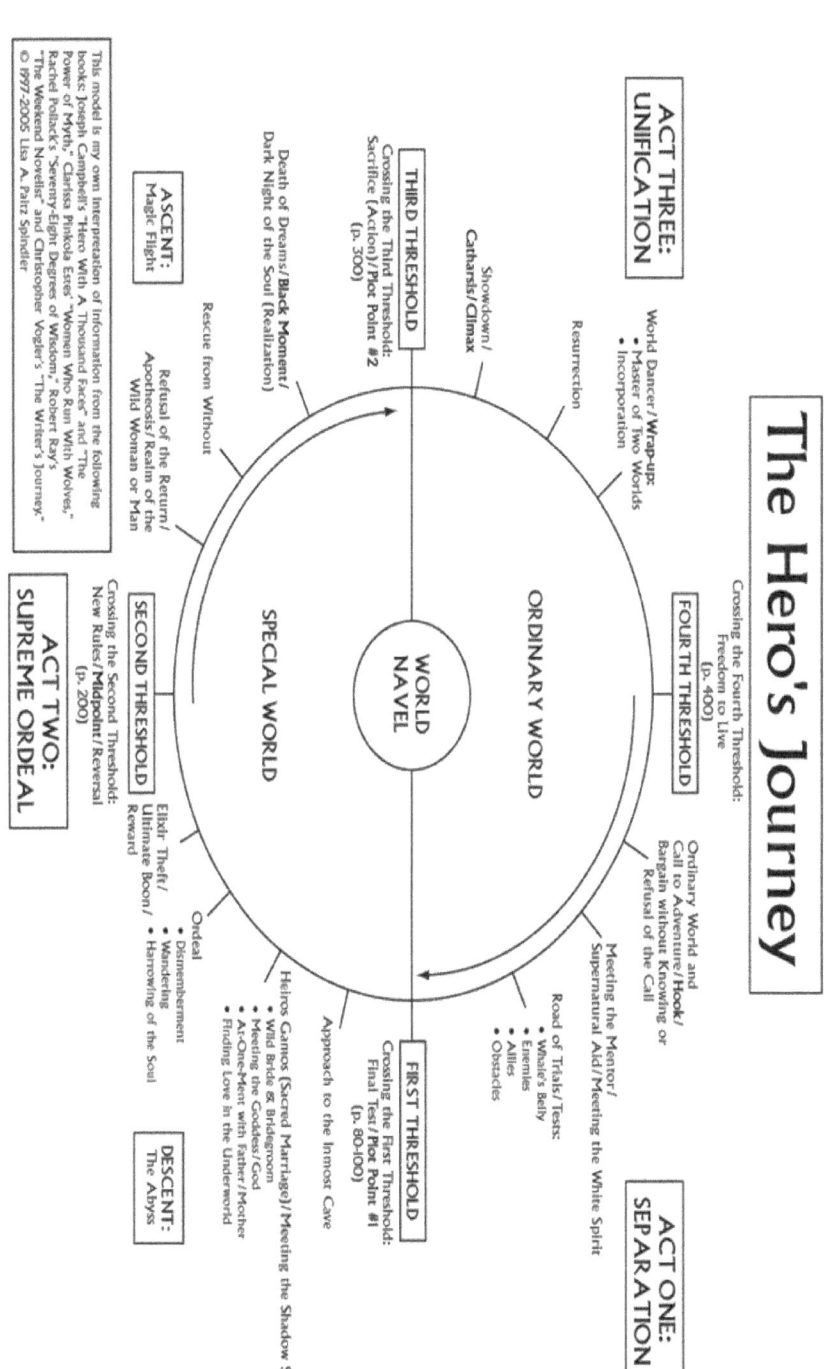

NINE CIRCLES OF THE ANGELIC ONES.

Out-of-body explorer Robert Monroe realized that the "locales" (planes) he visited had "rings" (sub-planes). He used the term "rings" rather than "sub planes" because the most natural shape in the universe is the sphere. Stars and planets are obviously spherical, but so too are galaxies and solar systems - the physical matter may be concentrated into a flat disc but the dark matter and dark energy (the subtle energy-matter of higher planes) forms a protective spherical "halo" around all galaxies and solar systems. So the planes, rather then being flat are actually a series of concentric spheres.

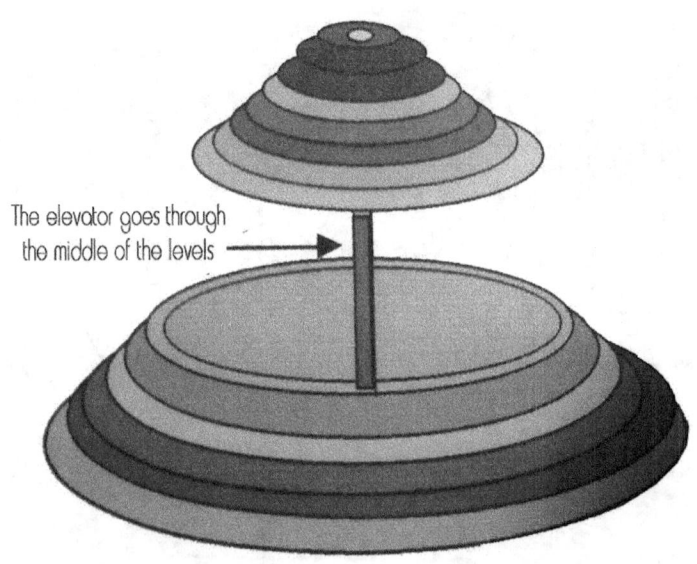

The elevator goes through the middle of the levels

Place 33, Secrets of Universal Truths Revealed

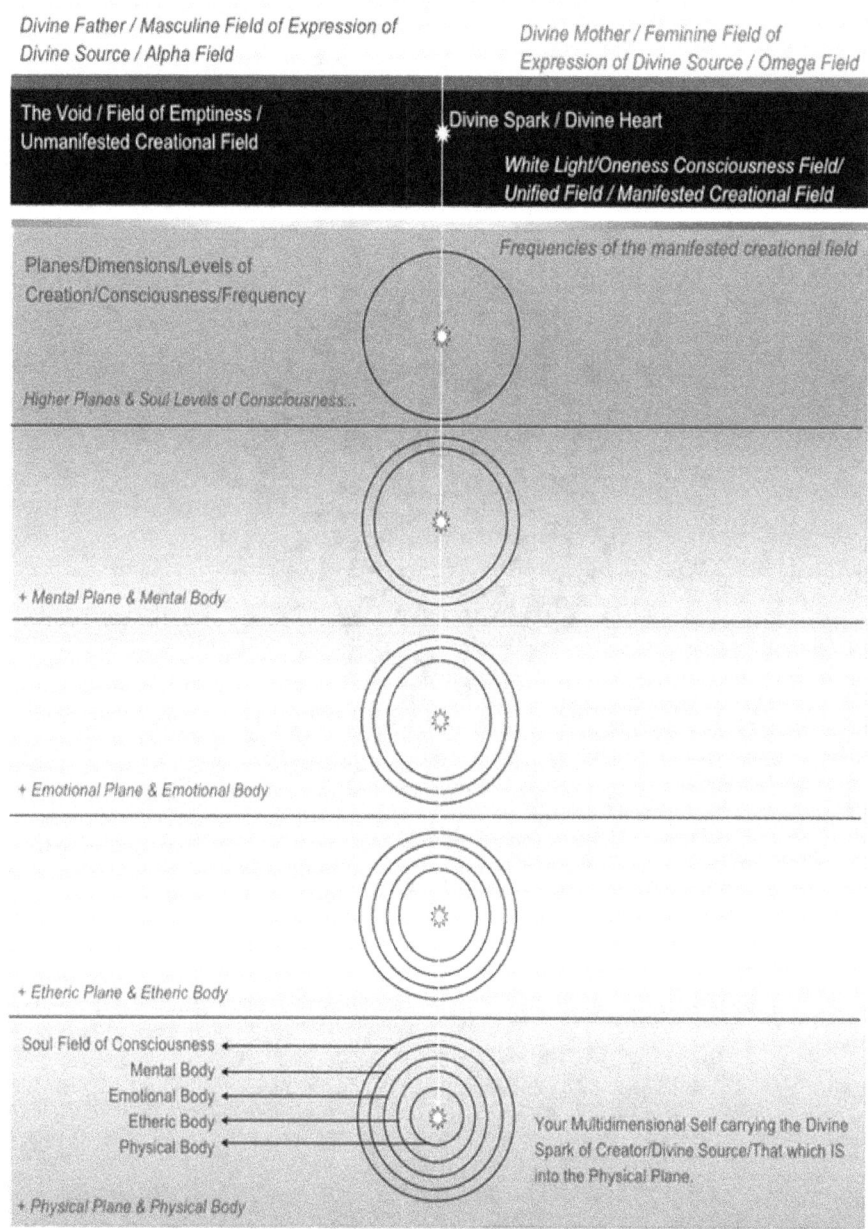

Once we become aware of the possible types of thoughts that the mind creates at different times in the span of a particular day, then we are in a position to keep a check on our thoughts.

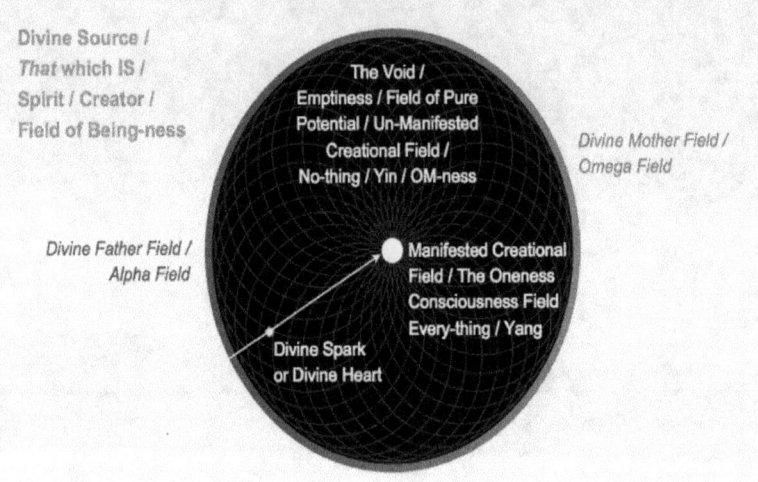

Now more than ever human beings are becoming aware that they are living as 'spirit in matter'.

EMANATIONIST COSMOLOGY

The Emanationist positionf then, is based on, not a single Creator-Created Dichotomy, but rather on a series or "hierarchy" of realities or "Worlds", arranged vertically.

Each of the levels of reality in the Emanationist Cosmology could be termed a "World".

Each higher world:

•Generates the one below it through a process of emanation, and each therefore stands in the position of "God" or "Creator" to the level or grade below it. Thus, creation is not creation out of nothing, but creation out of the being of the higher hypostasis.

Each of the levels or stages in this "spectrum" or "great chain of being" has its own specific characteristics. So you could speak of the psychic world (or astral plane), the angelic world, the archangelic world, the Divine world, and so on; hierarchy upon hierarchy, world upon world, a kind of epiphany or manifestation of the Divine; all looking downwards to matter, and also looking upwards to the godhead.

Sherilyn Bridget Avalon

New Paradigm Shift
Smoother Energy

Place 33, Secrets of Universal Truths Revealed

Don't worry...you get it, when you get it!

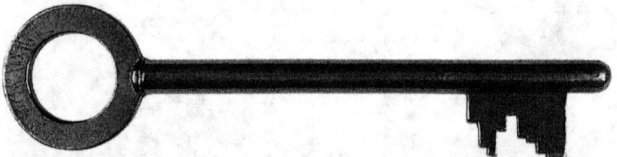

Whenever you find a key on the page
that reveals important information.

Place 33, Secrets of Universal Truths Revealed

Reviews:

Looking forward to book 2. It's weird how that while reading your book, my therapist is also talking about self-truth and ego. Also while reading and listening to music the word matrix came up in your text and in lyrics of song at the same time. Coincidence? I think not.

-Heather Beiber

In Part 2 it's one of the most detailed after-death communications ever recorded. The Afterlife of Joseph Campbell takes you on an unprecedented journey into the mysteries of life beyond death.

-Lisa Bernal

The wait is over. Place 33 is over here! Thrilling and entertaining, like the experience on a crazy roller coaster.

-Lydia Gillespie

Thrilling in the extreme, Place 33 is a definite page-flipper.

-Cosmic Archetypal Journal

Sherilyn Bridget Avalon

Children's Book Review
By Sherilyn Bridget Avalon

**Get it on Amazon or Barnes & Noble
Or Place 33.org**

Place 33, Secrets of Universal Truths Revealed

Love is the fire

Love is the fire
From whence we all came
Since all is sorrowful
Love is no game

The stronger the love
The more the pain
In tribute to you mother
And all before us

For we are the givers
And to us shall we know
Where all have come from
And where we all go

To Angie

Join us at our
Workshops & Webinars
Ascensions.us©

www.SherilynBridgetAvalon.com

www.Place33.org

Awaken Ascension Evolution

www.Ascensions.us

Place 33, Secrets of Universal Truths Revealed

Place 33, Touched By Angie, Book 2

Sherilyn Bridget Avalon

**With Love from
My Crazy Loving Family**

Place 33, Secrets of Universal Truths Revealed

www.ingramcontent.com/pod-product-compliance
Lightning Source LLC
Chambersburg PA
CBHW071904290426
44110CB00013B/1272